Cold Feet

The Complete Companion

Cold Feet
The Complete Companion

Rupert Smith

GRANADA

COLD FEET is a Granada Television Production

First published by Granada Media 2003
An imprint of Andre Deutsch Ltd
In association with Granada Media Ltd
20 Mortimer Street
London
WIT 3JW

A catalogue record for this book is available from the British Library.

ISBN: 0 233 00999 X

Designed by Tanya Devonshire-Jones
Project Editor: Gillian Holmes
Jacket design: Jeremy Southgate
Production: Lisa Moore

Photographs reproduced courtesy of Granada Media

Printed in Italy by Eurolitho S.p.A.

Contents

A few words from
Mike Bullen

(WRITER)

Mike Bullen spent the mid–nineties watching American TV and American movies and wondering why there was nothing with the same strong storytelling and production values on British television.

'I'd been thinking about films like *When Harry Met Sally*, and TV shows like *Hill Street Blues*, *The Simpsons* and *Frasier*, where the storytelling is so strong, and it frustrated me that British TV seemed to be lagging behind in that department. All those American shows were on big networks, they were anchored firmly in their genres, but they played with the genre. They seemed very sophisticated in the way they changed point of view, they way the characters related with the stories. British drama, in comparison, seemed to be rooted either in the Ken Loach, kitchen-sink tradition, or was way up the other end in *Brideshead Revisited* country. I wanted to do something that was for my generation and my class middle-class people in their 30s and 40s, basically. That group of people seemed unserved by most British drama. The soaps are obsessed with the working class, and costume dramas portray the lives of the rich. There was nothing in between.'

Bullen already had strong links with the Granada drama department; hed submitted a script entitled *My Perfect Match*, which was produced as a one-off drama starring Con O'Neill and Saskia Reeves (with John Thomson in a proto-Pete role). 'From the start I worked with Christine Langan, and it was Christine who encouraged me to do more. I was keen to do a boy-meets-girl story from the point of view of both sexes, where you got both of them presenting their take on the affair, and the humour would come out of the difference between the two. That was the genesis of *Cold Feet*. Christine and I had the same ambitions for the show: we wanted to emulate the quality of American drama, but to create something with a contemporary, British setting. It sounds obvious now, but there was nothing else on British television at the time that was doing that.'

Cold Feet started out as the story of one couple, Adam and Rachel, but it swiftly broadened out to an ensemble piece. 'I ended up writing about me and my friends, basically,' says Bullen. 'All the characters are drawn from real life. They're real people. Seven years ago, I was in the same position that Adam was in I'd been through a string of short-term relationships, and I was desperate to find Ms Right. Pete was based on my

best mate Mark, who I'd known since the age of 11. Jenny was the wife of another mate of ours, and so on. After we'd made the pilot, all my mates came and met their TV counterparts even David! The real David, the guy that he's based on, thinks he's the hero of the show, which is lucky for me. I know a lot of people think David is a buffoon, but deep down he's the

'I wanted to do something that was for my generation and my class.'

soundest of the lot of them. And yes, all those people are still my friends. They're heroes in their own offices.

People pull their legs about what 'they' have been up to on TV the night before, but I think they enjoy it.'

Even when Bullen wrote the pilot, he always envisaged *Cold Feet* as a series. 'It was a balancing act. The pilot had to be complete in itself, but I was consciously trying to set up a group of characters that could go places together. The trouble was, too many people saw the pilot as a great one-off and just thought I should leave it at that. ITV took a long time to commission the series. At the time ITV was a very different place from what it is now, and there was a general perception that *Cold Feet* was really a BBC show that had somehow found its way on to commercial television. That sounds ridiculous now, because the two channels have

'If the pilot hadn't won the Golden Rose at Montreux, things could have worked out very differently.'

become totally interchangeable, but at the time *Cold Feet* was very unusual for ITV and it sat rather awkwardly in their portfolio of dramas. They weren't sure what they had on their hands, and they weren't at all sure if they wanted it. So while they were making their minds up, both BBC1 and Channel 4 had made overtures to us. If the pilot hadn't won the Golden Rose at Montreux, things could have worked out very differently.'

As it was, the pilot got off to a shaky start. The transmission was delayed by 20 minutes because there was a big smash-up at the Grand Prix, and live sports coverage over-ran. 'As a result the pilot didnt finish till 11.20pm, by which time only my mother was watching. Michael Schumacher nearly destroyed *Cold Feet* before it even started. And the ratings were bad. Andy Harries, the head of drama at Granada, just said 'forget it'. Then things changed. We won at Montreux, and David Liddiment came in as the head of entertainment at ITV and he commissioned a series. The repeat screening of the pilot had done well and by that time, of course, we were 'the award-winning *Cold Feet*' and so I finally got to write some more.'

'Montreux was a strange experience. ITV had never done well in the comedy category, but it so happened that year that there was a dearth of other material so we were put up for it. I was sick in bed with flu at the time, so Andy Harries went over. We won in our category, and Andy flew home, because he didn't think there was any chance we'd win the overall prize. So then he had to get straight back on a plane and go back to collect the Golden Rose.'

It was a fraught time for Bullen, who was still holding down his day job as a presenter for the BBC World Service. 'Radio had been my career up to that point, while I waited for my TV work to take off. I'd produced and presented for eight years, and I was quite content with it. Then the call came about the series. I was delighted, of course, but the euphoria and relief were quickly replaced by a feeling of 'Oh shit! Now Ive got to write six episodes!'. And *Cold Feet* was only my second script; it's not as if I was a really experienced screenwriter. By the third series I felt I'd mastered it, but the first series was a very steep learning curve. I had no confidence. All credit goes to Christine Langan, really: she was the script editor as well as the producer, and she made sure that the scripts were as strong as possible.'

Bullen stayed at the World Service right through the first series, then cut back from three weekly shows to one for the second series. 'I didn't totally give up radio till the third series, by which time I was confident that I had a career in television. Up to that point I felt I needed another string to my bow, because the recommissions were always very precarious and I

could have easily been out of a job. I moved out of London and went to live in Cambridge, where I was writing two full days a week, and at evenings and weekends. The relief of finally giving up radio and going full time on *Cold Feet* was immense; up to that point my life just hadn't been my own.'

The first series quickly garnered an army of fans who rooted strongly for the characters and put pressure on Bullen to give them a happy ending. 'But I was always determined to end

'Oh shit! Now I've got to write six episodes!'

it on a downbeat note. That's the point of *Cold Feet*, as far as I'm concerned, that mixture of happy and sad. So I had Rachel leaving Adam in Manchester and going down to London to have the baby. It would have been so easy for them to be reconciled, and we played with that idea in a fantasy sequence right at the end of the last show, just before reality kicked in and she left Piccadilly Station. A lot of people were disappointed, but it was true to life. And being true to life is what got us through five series.

The first series was very funny on the surface, but underneath it was

Mike Bullen

quite bleak and that's what people responded to. It was hard to pull it off, but it worked. When Rachel left Adam, my sister rang me up in tears and said "Oh Mike, how could you?" That was exactly the response I was striving for.'

It was during the second series that *Cold Feet* broke through to a wider audience. 'I started going to parties and people had actually heard of the show. During the first series, if I mentioned *Cold Feet* people just looked blank. During the second series, it was hit and miss, but at least people knew what I was talking about. It wasn't 'til the third series that I was confident that people would be impressed. That's the litmus test for me, if real people have heard of it. As a writer I'm quite out of touch with popular culture. I don't work in an office so I don't get those water-cooler conversations. So I only got it anecdotally, at parties and through friends. Being a writer, you should have your finger on the pulse, but in fact you're often the last person to find out what's actually going on in the real world.'

By the time the third series had been commissioned, Bullen felt confident with his creation and started to enjoy himself a bit more. 'I just knew the characters so well by then that I knew how they would react to any given situation. So writing dialogue was easy; what got harder was coming up with situations for the characters to be in. I always say that the characters in *Cold Feet* are real, but the situations aren't. Obviously I've drawn to some extent on things that have happened to me and my friends, but nobody could have that much happening to them in one life. In the pilot we'd given audiences a very big story arc, we'd covered a lot of ground in 50 minutes, and we had to keep up that kind of pace. If you're telling stories at that rate, you eat up a hell of a lot of material. It's not like an art movie, where you can dwell on the telling details. We had to keep up a cracking pace, and that's really draining.

There were some very strange

> ### 'We had to keep up a cracking pace, and that's really draining.'

practical decisions that had to be made. For instance, at the end of series one we decided we had to get rid of Rachel's baby, otherwise we'd start the second series with all three couples having children, and that would have been terribly limiting in terms of storylines. So we killed off that child for purely narrative reasons! We had to become very heartless, but when you're writing drama you basically play God with your characters. By the fourth series, we were getting desperate for material.'

And so, says Bullen, the fifth series of *Cold Feet* is definitely the last. 'We've got to stop now before we

'You know it's time to stop when you start considering an alien abduction plot.'

start repeating ourselves. *Cold Feet* has always been about ordinary lives, and if it went on any further we'd have to start putting the characters into extraordinary situations. You know it's time to stop when you start considering an alien abduction plot.'

Finishing off his characters turned out to be easier than Bullen expected. 'At the end of every series, I always had to feel that a line had been drawn, that we could finish it there and then with a real sense of closure. When I was writing the fifth series, which I knew was really going to be the last one, I fretted about the ending for so long that in the event it was one of the easier ones to do. Once I'd taken the decision to kill Rachel, everything else fell into place. *Cold Feet* has always been about the health of the characters' inner selves, and at the end of the line they all

know where they're going, even if they're not entirely happy with it.'

Such was his involvement with the show that Bullen was tempted, on occasion, to involve himself in the production side. 'I was very interested in directing a few episodes, but I thought better of it. I'm a writer. Let the directors direct. I would have been inadequate. It's tempting to wade in if you think that they haven't understood a line, but I tend to keep my distance. Apart from anything else, shooting is so boring. I couldn't stand it for more than a couple of days.'

Bullen did succumb to a Hitchcock-like desire to appear in his own creations, however. 'I had cameos in several of the episodes. In the pilot,

'I fretted about the ending for so long that in the event it was one of the easier ones to do.'

I was the bad actor in the pretentious fringe play that Adam takes Rachel to when he's trying to get her into bed. I was wearing a loin cloth, covered in white body paint and I did some dreadful mime. In the first series, I'm the neighbour who watches in horror as Adam pegs out Baby Adam on the washing line. I was the husband of the

Japanese woman at Baby Adam's christening. One of the best ones never made it to the screen it was my one and only nude scene. I just wanted to see what it was like! Adam and David were in the changing rooms at the squash club, and I was getting changed in the background. All the others were firemen, so I didn't look too impressive in comparison. But the lenses of the cameras kept steaming up, so it had to be cut. I made an impression, though. When I was getting off the catering bus, one of the make-up girls came up to me and said "We've seen your todger!"

Bullen did involve himself in the editing process; the scripts were so complicated, with their deployment of fantasy and flashback, that he wanted

'A film is made three times: it's written, it's shot and it's edited.'

to be sure that the editors were getting it right. 'A film is made three times: it's written, it's shot and it's edited. My narrative is quite dense, and I was worried that the editors wouldn't get it but of course they did. I learned to keep my distance. There's always more than one way of delivering a line, or of doing a cut, and they know what they're doing. It was

innovative at the time: we had characters stopping in mid-speech and looking at the camera, that sort of thing. It felt very fresh. Now everyone's doing it, and it's expected of us, but back at the start the only other show that was playing around with narrative in that way was *Ally McBeal*. I don't know which came first.'

As with all long-running series, *Cold Feet* has had to overcome its fair share of practical problems. This caused a few headaches for the writer. 'When we were working on the adoption storyline in series four, Helen Baxendale was actually pregnant. We knew that from the outset, and we'd planned to introduce Rachel's pregnancy into the sixth episode of that series, by which time she and Adam had adopted a child. But Helen started showing a lot earlier than expected, and so we had to bring the pregnancy plot forward to the fourth episode. That, of course, derailed the whole adoption storyline, but the art of these things is to turn every problem into an opportunity. We worked that into the story — Rachel got pregnant and wasn't allowed to adopt. It gave a great poignancy to that series. The scenes in which Adam met the little girl they were going to adopt were very powerful and then she was taken away from them. I was very keen to show the social worker in a positive light, because they usually get such a hard time from the press and the media. I showed her as a woman who had to take a very hard decision in the best interests of a child, and who was deeply affected by it. We showed her bursting into tears after she'd given the bad news to Adam and Rachel. It would have been easy to cut that scene, but it meant a lot to me. Social workers are human too!'.

Like the rest of the *Cold Feet* crew, Mike Bullen has grown up with the show, and has ploughed his own experience back into the scripts. 'I was 35 when I wrote the pilot. I met and married Lisa between the pilot and the first series. Our first child, Maggie, was born in 1997, when the first

'A lot of the material about conception and parenthood in the first series came from my own experience.'

series was going out, then Rachel came in 1999. A lot of the material about conception and parenthood in the first series came from my own experience. Pete's anxieties about being a father were mine. I thought

fatherhood would be an idyllic dream, but the truth is that it's a mixed blessing. It takes away a large chunk of your life.

I always used *Cold Feet* as a way of

'I always used Cold Feet as a way of exploding myths about love, family life, sex.'

exploding myths about love, family life, sex. There's a line that Karen says to Mark about how putting your socks back on after sex is God's way of making you feel guilty. I wanted to write about sex in a way that debunks the TV fantasy. Sex on TV is usually wonderful, but let's face it, in real life it's not always that great. At least, I don't think it's just me.'

Now *Cold Feet* is a closed book, and Bullen has moved with his wife and daughters to Australia. 'The Australian episodes at the end of series four were all part of my campaign to get an Australian visa. All my wife's family are out here, and it's a much better place to bring the children up. We live north of Sydney in a beach suburb called Avalon. It's beautiful. Australia is very 1950s in some ways. They still have Tupperware parties where I live.'

Pilot

30 March 1997 ⓢ 1 episode

It ended up winning the **Golden Rose** of Montreux and initiating a series that would run for five years, but at the time of its first broadcast the pilot episode of **Cold Feet** was very nearly a one-off. Originally scheduled for 10pm, it was broadcast 40 minutes late. Audience figures were dented, and critical reaction the next day was muted to say the least. But there was something about the show that impressed the people who saw it - even if there weren't very many of them. This was something new, a **glimpse** into a life that was at once familiar and strange. Audiences recognised the milieu of bars, offices and flats from their own lives - and for the first time the **thirtysomethings** of the late 1990s had a show that they could call their own.

The pilot focused on Adam and his **courtship** of Rachel. The rest of the cast were very much in supporting roles, a **comic counterpoint** to the main action. David and Karen were the established married couple, their lives drifting into premature middle-aged dullness. Pete and Jenny were acting out another drama - parenthood. Adam was ready for neither of those things, and it's hardly surprising that, between the rock of marriage and the hard place of parenthood, he started to get **Cold Feet**.

Even though this was Mike Bullen's first **Cold Feet** script, it encapsulated all the elements that were to make the show a hit. Stories were told in **flashback**, characters commented on each other's narratives, there were **fantasies** and moments of **pure lunacy**. And, to cap it all, James Nesbitt took all his clothes off and stuck a rose up his **bum**.

Pilot

Rachel and Adam collide in a car park ... Karen's finding it hard to cope as a working mother ... Pete and Jenny are trying for a baby

Adam Williams is a serial monogamist whose current relationship has lasted three months. Rachel Bradley has a freshly-pierced belly button and a nice boyfriend called Simon. But, within five minutes of the start of the Cold Feet pilot, both have been cut adrift and set on a collision course that will bring them head to head, or at least bumper to bumper, in a Tesco car park in Greater Manchester.

The first ever episode of *Cold Feet* does a neat job of introducing us to three interlocking couples. While Adam and Rachel are courting in their own unique way, we meet David and Karen – well-to-do, middle-class parents of the very demanding Joshua – and Pete and Jenny, a scruffy married couple who are trying, with varying degrees of enthusiasm, for a child. Jenny's life is controlled by her menstrual cycles, which she has charted out with frightening accuracy on a computer spreadsheet; Pete's under orders to perform in bed whenever conception seems most likely. So it's hardly surprising that Jenny fails to see the funny side when Pete rolls in, several pints later, after a lads' night out with Adam, unable to walk in a straight line, let alone father a child. And to make matters worse, Adam – freshly chucked by his latest girlfriend – has missed his last bus and wants to kip on the couch.

Karen has the opposite problem: she's got the baby, but she's having to cope with it singlehandedly while David spends more and more time away from home. Karen wants a nanny, David won't hear of it. 'Motherhood does not end at birth,' he says, pompously. 'Nor fatherhood at conception,' she snaps back.

Soon Karen has yet another person to look after: Rachel's been dumped by Simon, who seems to prefer a lucrative contract in Hong Kong to a lifetime of domestic bliss with Rachel, he gets a bowl of profiteroles emptied into his lap by way of thanks. The girls comfort themselves with the

Cold Facts

🌀 James Nesbitt wasn't quite naked for the rose-up-the-bum scene; he was wearing a small posing pouch to cover his modesty. The rose had the thorns removed and was held in place by sellotape.

🌀 The song that Adam sang in the original script was Nilsson's 'Without You', but was replaced at the last moment by 'I've Got You Under My Skin'.

Can Adam win Rachel's love? Or, more to the point, will Rachel be able to decide between these two?

thought that all men are bastards – an opinion that only seems to be reinforced when Rachel's car gets bumped at the supermarket. She locks horns with the other driver – a man, of course – only to discover, after a minute of heated banter, that he's rather an attractive proposition. They exchange telephone numbers. His name? Adam Williams. She can hardly wait for him to call.

But Adam, being Adam, loses Rachel's number and starts staking out Tesco in the vain hope of running into her again. Rachel, disillusioned by the hopeless dates Karen's lining up for her, swallows her pride and decides to make the first move. And so begins a long, cautious and (for Adam, at least) frustrating period of courtship. They go to galleries together. They have meals and drinks. They see films. Adam, climbing the walls with lust, seeks advice from his best mate Pete. Take her out, says Pete, get a few drinks down her neck, get her back to your place – and bingo. 'Don't you think she might suspect?' asks Jenny. 'You didn't,' deadpans Pete.

And so, after a ghastly four hours watching existential Spanish drama in a small (but crucially local) theatre, Adam manages to get Rachel back home and into bed... And from that point on, he can hardly wait to tell the world all about it. Jenny and Pete, exhausted from their fruitless attempts to conceive, spend hour after hour listening to Adam banging on about his new-found happiness.

It's all going well; too well, perhaps. So, Rachel puts Adam to the test. If I was lost, would you search the world to find me? Of course. Would you fight a giant for my hand? Yes! Would you stand stark bollock naked in the street serenading me, with a rose stuck up your bum? 'Ask me one on sport,' says Adam. But it's duly noted...

The honeymoon period is intense but short-lived. Adam, goaded by Pete's gloomy warnings about the perils of monogamy, starts to get cold feet. He hates Rachel's friends, particularly David, who takes great delight in exposing Adam's shortcomings during social occasions. He's terrified of fatherhood, and runs a mile at the merest hint of maternal instinct. Yes, the time has come for the man to demand a little more 'space' – and so, on Pete's advice, he engineers a futile row with Rachel, packs his bags and moves out of her flat (although, according to Adam, he had never moved in).

This is very bad timing. No sooner has he slammed the door than Rachel is opening it to a contrite Simon, back from Hong Kong and very eager to start where they left off. Rachel, on the rebound, takes Simon back, but also finds it hard to resist a repentant Adam. For a few weeks, much to Karen's astonishment, she's seeing them both, trying to make her mind up – something that Rachel Bradley has never been good at.

By the end of the show, the three storylines come to a head. Karen's taken the nanny business into her own hands, storming into David's office and giving him an ultimatum (which slimy David tries to pass off on his amused colleagues as an exercise in role playing and negotiation). Jenny and Pete are emerging from the hell of fertility tests and spend much of their time hunkered down over pregnancy tests. Adam, meanwhile, decides that he really loves Rachel and is willing to fight for her – and off he goes to find her.

After a couple of false starts, he finally tracks her down in Simon's flat, prepared to fight, man-to-man, for the hand of his true love. Sadly for Adam, Simon is a karate expert, and chucks him down the stairs. Well, he's searched the world, he's fought the giant – now all that remains is to stick the rose up his bum. And so, stark naked in the street, he serenades Rachel with a heartfelt rendition of 'I've Got You Under My Skin'...

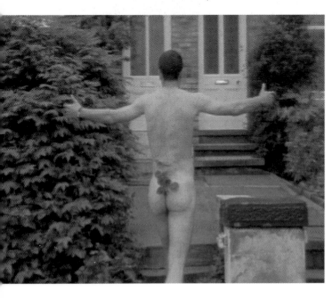

And it works. Adam gets his girl, Karen gets her nanny, and Jenny gets pregnant. The sun sets over three very happy couples in Didsbury – for now, at least. But their stories had only just begun...

Adam proves his love.

The gang in the early days.

SCENE 22 MORNING DAY 2
SET EXT SUPERMARKET CARPARK

ADAM: RACHEL:

ADAM SIGHS DEEPLY. HE ANGRILY FLINGS OPEN HIS CAR DOOR AND
CLIMBS OUT. RACHEL IS ALREADY INSPECTING THE DAMAGE.

ADAM: (ANGRILY) What the hell were you doing?!

Rachel: (EQUALLY FURIOUS) Me! It's you who reversed without
looking.

Adam: At about five miles an hour! You didn't have to ram
me.

Rachel: (INDIGNANT) Excuse me, but whose car is touching
whose?!

Adam: Oh terrific! A woman driver with a woman's logic!

Rachel: (STILL ANGRY) And a man with shit for brains.

THE VEHEMENCE OF THIS ATTACK LEAVES ADAM MOMENTARILY
SPEECHLESS. RACHEL PRESSES HOME HER ADVANTAGE.

Rachel: Tell me, were you starved of oxygen at birth?

RATHER THAN BEING OFFENDED, ADAM FINDS THAT HE'S AMUSED BY
RACHEL'S FIGHTING SPIRIT. HIS ANGER DISAPPEARS.

Adam: (JOUSTING) And who was your driving instructor?
Stevie Wonder?

RACHEL REALISES HE'S PLAYING WITH HER. SHE RESPONDS IN
KIND.

Rachel: At least I had one.

Adam: (MOCK SINCERELY) How that man must have suffered.

Rachel: Actually it was a woman.

ADAM HOLDS BACK FROM THE OBVIOUS RIPOSTE. INSTEAD HE

SMILES, OFFERING A DRAW. THEY EACH REGARD THE OTHER A
MOMENT, THEIR ANIMOSITY REPLACED BY THE BEGINNINGS OF
ATTRACTION.

Adam: (TAKING OUT HIS WALLET) Look., there really isn't any
damage, but er, maybe we should swap phone numbers. (HAND-
ING RACHEL HIS CARD) You know, just in case you want to get
in touch with your insurance.

Rachel: (READING CARD) 'Systems analyst'. What's that when
it's at home?

Adam: (SHRUGS) A job.

RACHEL LOOKS AT HIM, RECOGNISING A KINDRED SPIRIT. A BEAT

Adam: Erm, aren't I supposed to take yours as well?

Rachel: Oh, yes, er I don't have a pen on me.

ADAM LOOKS THWARTED. THEY STAND IN EMBARRASSED SILENCE A
MOMENT, NEITHER KNOWING WHAT TO DO. SUDDENLY, RACHEL IS
STRUCK BY AN IDEA. USING HER FINGER, SHE SCRAWLS THE NUM-
BERS 291 0349 IN THE DUST ON THE BACK WINDOW OF ADAM'S CAR.

Adam: Right, well, maybe see you around.

Rachel: Oh, don't worry. I'll be on the look-out for you.

ADAM NODS, AMUSED, AND TURNS BACK TOWARDS HIS CAR.

Rachel: Oh, one other thing?

Adam: (EXPECTANTLY) Yes?

Rachel: Can I have your parking space?

ADAM SMILES

Adam Williams

(JAMES NESBITT)

Adam Williams is one big bundle of contradictions. On first acquaintance, he seems like an archetypal Jack the Lad – an image he's keen to cultivate. In his time he's been a great drinker and a great shagger, or at least that's what he'd like you to believe. In his fantasy life, he sees himself as a Belfast James Bond, who seduces women in between feats of derring-do, while contriving to look very cool at all times. The reality, however, is very different. All Adam really wants in life is to settle down with one woman and lead a normal, placid family life. The difficulty in reconciling these two urges gets him into scrapes – but really, when push comes to shove, what Adam wants is stability and security. And Rachel.

Rachel changes Adam from a boy into a man. When they first meet, Adam is rushing from one girlfriend to another, convinced that he's enjoying himself but dimly conscious of the need to settle down with someone special. At first he pursues her like he would any other chance encounter: after all, a flirtatious meeting over a dented bumper in a Tesco car park isn't the most auspicious beginning to a life-long relationship. But he soon realises there's more to Rachel than that. It's not just that they have a good sex life – although that's very important to Adam, whose high libido needs a lot of maintenance. Rachel is just his ideal match: a woman who loves life, who's reckless and impetuous, and complex enough to keep Adam on his toes. He could never settle down with a dull partner, and, much as he complains about Rachel's strange whims, they're what keep the relationship fresh.

There's only one thing that stands between Adam and happiness, and that's a great fear of commitment. When he's working on his relationship with Rachel, it's two steps forward, one step back. He wants them to build a life together, but he constantly gets cold feet. Faced with the prospect of moving in together, he squirms and prevaricates and finds a thousand reasons not to do it – although of course it's what he wants more than anything else. His insane avoidance tactics

Loves
♡ Freedom
♡ Football
♡ Kids
♡ Rachel

Hates
۞ Commitment
۞ Doctors
۞ Dullness
۞ Decisions

(cloned wardrobes, anyone?) just show that he's fooling nobody but himself. Every time there's a major life decision to be made – starting a family, for instance, or getting married – Adam rushes forward, takes fright and rushes back. Anyone who's willing to take that on has to have a great deal of patience.

The key to all this, of course, lies in Adam's childhood. As a boy growing up in Northern Ireland he was popular and well-liked, good at football, attractive to the opposite sex. His confidence took one hell of a knock, however, when his father left his mother, and witheld all communication with his son. Adam never knew what had happened – he only knew that his father had rejected him, and that his mother forbade him to have any contact. The split was never discussed, and for years the air of secrecy and denial festered within Adam, leaving him suspicious of commitment and cynical about marriage. In his young adulthood, he convinced himself that marriage is for suckers, and that he can breeze through life taking his pleasures where he finds them. That's all very well in his 20s, but as he moves into his 30s he finds that he wants more out of life – he wants what a permanent, committed relationship can give him. But his great role model for family life was a disaster. Little does Rachel know what she's taking on...

Despite his childhood problems, Adam's not an over-complex individual. He doesn't spend hours brooding over problems, and can usually see the way ahead, even if it takes him a while. Any negative aspects to his character are balanced out by a surfeit of confidence; he's had enough success with women in his life to convince him that he's attractive, and he's always found it easy to make friends. Everyone who meets Adam thinks he's fun and easy-going – but, as his old friends will tell you, there's a less attractive side to Adam's confidence. He's obsessed by winning; you only have to play poker with him to find that out. He always assumes that he's the coolest, smartest and sexiest man in any situation, which makes it hard for other men to get close to him. Pete's stuck by him over the years because, basically, Pete's a bit of a doormat, a submissive yin to Adam's dominant yang. Adam's always stealing Pete's friends, nicking his interests and hobbies, even alienating his girlfriends and ultimately his wife – and Pete puts up with it because Adam is loyal to him in other ways. And it's quite clear that a lot of Adam's self-confidence is built on his relationship with Pete. Without Pete to compare himself with, Adam would be a lot less cocky.

His relationships with women are very different. Adam really likes women, which explains why they find him so attractive. His great confidante in life is Jenny; if he has real problems, he'll pour his heart out to her and will follow her advice. He would never do that with Pete, except in extreme situations; to admit weakness to another man would entail a loss of face. But with women, Adam drops the machismo and allows himself to be vulnerable. It's difficult for him, and he finds the idea threatening – but, ultimately, it's part of his growing up. When he faces the worst things in life – cancer, relationship problems, bereavement – he can (eventually) drop his defences and let his true feelings show. It's not easy for him, but without that shell of cocky confidence, Adam would not be Adam.

'Trust me. I'm Irish.'

ADAM WILLIAMS

MIKE BULLEN ON *Adam*

The Adam of the Pilot was based on me in the period of my life before I met my wife. I was going from one relationship to another, desperately looking for Ms Right. Adam's a man-child, someone who's never fully grown up, and he has that childlike disregard for other people's feelings. Fundamentally he's a good bloke, but he can be very insensitive and selfish. I never did fully work out Adam's biography. We knew that he grew up with Pete, but then we had to explain why he had such a heavy Irish accent, so we invented something about a childhood in Northern Ireland and frequent visits back there during the school holidays. I'm sure we made lots of gaffes, but then **Cold Feet** was full of gaffes. Karen, for instance, had two birthdays.

Adam's relationship with Jenny was always close.

James Nesbitt

(Adam Williams)

There's little doubt that the biggest star to emerge from *Cold Feet* is James Nesbitt. Adam was always the centre of the show, the character closest to writer Mike Bullen's heart – and Nesbitt's performance seemed to sum up the *Cold Feet* appeal. 'It was clear to me from the word go that this was a brilliant script,' he says. 'From the first moment I read the pilot I was absolutely desperate to do it. I knew the director, Declan Lowney, through a mutual friend, and I did everything I could to get a meeting with him. And once I got an audition, I told them that I wanted to read it in my own accent, even though Adam was never written as an Irishman. Adam was based on Mike himself – or at least that was how he would have liked to have seen himself at that time. But it felt important to me to do it in an Irish accent, because I could see this was a chance to present a Northern Irish character with absolutely no political baggage. That's rare in contemporary drama.'

Nesbitt got the part, and the necessary rewrites were made to acknowledge Adam's new-found Irishness. 'We did the pilot, and everyone was very happy with that, and I was convinced the show had a lot of potential, but then there was a long, long wait. It didn't get shown for a long time, and even when it was shown it went out at a funny time, late at night. Then it won the Golden Rose at Montreux, and we got commissioned for a series. That was the most exciting time, because we'd waited so long but we always had faith in it. The original pitch was that it was taking six ordinary lives and making them extraordinary, and that's what *Cold Feet* has always done. It's not just to do with the techniques of flashback and fantasy, although that helps a lot. I think it's just the degree of insight that Mike brought to those everyday situations. He made audiences care about those characters, whatever they went through.'

Adam went through more than most, from his first chance meeting with Rachel in a car park right through to the final farewell in Port Meirion. 'Of course the characters go through more than most people,' says Nesbitt, 'because this is telly, and it has to be full of incident. But what's important about *Cold Feet* is that every single situation is real and plausible. There are never any ridiculous, outlandish storylines. At its core, it's a love story, and that's what keeps it real. Adam's journey is the same that most people of my generation have been on: he starts off as a bit of a lad's lad, drinking and chasing women, and then he meets someone and has to face up to the responsibilities of adulthood. He grows up a bit over the course of the show, like I have. But I think he remains, in essence, the same man: always a bit of a lad, a bit of a fool, vulnerable. Women find him attractive because they can see his faults. He's not as arrogant as he

In case you're wondering, Adam is being chased by a giant testicle.

might appear. And in the years that we've been making *Cold Feet*, the audience has grown up with Adam as well. That's why I'll be absolutely devastated when it's over. It's become so much part of all our lives, I don't know how we'll be able to say goodbye.'

Of course, the personal highpoint of *Cold Feet* for Nesbitt was the Irish trip. 'Originally they were going to film the stag night in Dublin, but I tried to talk them out of it. I just felt that Dublin had been done to death, and I persuaded them to go to the north, to the seaside round Portrush and Coleraine, where I grew up. To go back to my home town, where I grew up from the age of 11, to film outside my local bar with a crew of 60 and 1000 people watching, was really moving. I felt like the king of the world.'

There have been other highlights – storylines that were a challenge for the actors and rewarding in terms of audience feedback. 'I was very proud of the testicular cancer storyline; it was a good way of getting that message across, and now I'm a patron of Action Cancer in Northern Ireland. The same applies to the fertility storyline. But what really sticks out for me is the relationship between Adam and Rachel. That was what *Cold Feet* was always about for me, and Helen and I worked on that for five years. I'll miss it desperately. We didn't see each other socially, but we worked together for all that time and it's hard to let go of that. I really believed in that love story. Yes, they split up, they had their problems, but love was at the core of everything.'

Cold Feet's been good to James Nesbitt; in the last couple of years, he's been working almost non-stop in high-profile film and TV projects. 'But I've always fitted in other stuff. Right after the pilot I flew off to make Welcome to Sarajevo, and I've worked consistently ever since. *Cold Feet* has always been the focus; I have to fit other jobs in around the four months of each year that's been spent up in Manchester. *Murphy's Law* [Nesbitt's police thriller for BBC1] had to be filmed in two blocks to accommodate the final series of *Cold Feet*; everything else, like *Bloody Sunday*, has to be made in the down time. I'm in the fortunate position now that I've got a lot of offers on the table. Bloody Sunday did very

Adam and Rachel. Their love story is
at the heart of *Cold Feet*

well in the States, and there's stuff happening for me over there now. But it all
stems from *Cold Feet*. That's why I've always been happy to talk about the show,
because it's been good for all of us and I believe that it's a really good piece of
television. When it first came out, it was truly innovative. Nobody had used those
techniques of flashback and fantasy before. You see them everywhere now; there
are so many shows that owe a lot to *Cold Feet*. But we were the first.'

Nesbitt has another focus in his life as well now: his two daughters, Peggy and
Mary, were born during the run of *Cold Feet*. 'The changes that Adam's had have
mirrored the changes in my own life. When we first started the show, we had a
mad honeymoon period when we were all up in Manchester together, going out
every night, partying hard and having a ball. They were exciting times. But that's
calmed down a lot. I've got a family now, so I go down to London when I've got
time off to see them. The party days are over.'

Series 1

A year has passed. Adam and Rachel are celebrating their first anniversary, Pete and Jenny are expecting their first child, Karen and Rachel are getting used to their first nanny. And from that seemingly stable starting point, all hell breaks looose. With each episode, the gang comes up against the major stumbling blocks that beset modern relationships — sex, jealousy, exes, growing old, having kids. Rachel lets the first of many enormous cats out of the bag, revealing that she's already been married once and has never got a divorce. Things get worse when Kris, her ex-husband, turns up to discuss a divorce and stays to become an unwelcome third in the house. When Rachel discovers she's pregnant, she panics: the baby might not be Adam's. Only time will tell: if the child is black, it's Kris's. Torn between her desire to stay with Adam and the fear that their relationship can never survive the uncertainty, she flees to London…

Pete and Jenny, meanwhile, are finding it hard to adjust to parenthood. After six weeks without sex, Pete's climbing the walls — but when he finally gets the green light again he finds it hard to fancy a wife who's suddenly become a mother. But these domestic adjustments are put into sharp focus when, at Baby Adam's christening, Pete hears that his father has died.

For Karen and David, the problems are more practical. David's lost a lot of money in dodgy investments, and finds his sexual performance is suffering. But is a visit to a prostitute really the answer?

Series 1

Episode 1

Should Adam and Rachel move in together? Should Pete be reading all those books about childbirth? Should little Josh be potty trained already? All this pales into insignificance when Jenny goes into labour – and Pete goes missing

Several months have elapsed. Adam and Rachel are celebrating their first anniversary (at least, it's a year since they first had sex), and in honour of the occasion he's hired a scissor lift and a band of Mexican troubadours to serenade Rachel at work. Nice idea... shame the lift doesn't work properly and that the windows in Rachel's office are too thick for her to hear the strains of 'Guantanamera'. Some hours later, she walks out of the building to find him stuck up a lift, the Mexican boys still playing lustily away...

A typically over-the-top romantic gesture from Adam, sadly passes Rachel by.

Pete and Jenny are approaching a significant date as well: the birth. In the intervening months, Pete has changed from a diffident dad-to-be to an all-round expert and amateur gynaecologist. He's got an emergency bag packed and ready to go, he's worked out the best routes to the hospital and he's read every single book on childbirth. He even gets competitive during quizzes at Jenny's ante-natal

The peerless Ramona
with little Josh.

classes. Jenny, meanwhile, views the impending day with alternating terror and indifference.

Karen has won the nanny wars, and her household is now augmented by the lovely Ramona, a capable carer and an enthusiastic student of the English language. David, of course, does not appreciate her mangling of his mother tongue ('ten grin bottool hanking from the wool') and blames her for what he perceives to be Josh's intellectual shortcomings. According to David, his little boy should not only be potty trained, but should also be displaying signs of nascent genius at nursery. Instead, Josh is making a thorough nuisance of himself, punching other kids and generally being antisocial. David decides it's time he had a father's guidance – and takes to reading him financial reports as bedtime stories.

Adam and Rachel, like most new couples, are getting sick of living out of a suitcase at each other's flat – but Adam, clinging desperately to the last vestiges of his independence, is terrified by the idea of cohabitation. Finally, crushed by the humiliation of having to wear Rachel's pants to work, he suggests a brilliant compromise – 'Let's clone our wardrobes!'. Rachel agrees, to Karen's astonishment, but she has an ace up her sleeve. While Adam races round Marks and Spencers getting fresh shirts, socks and underwear, Rachel spends a very enjoyable three hours strolling round Manchester's designer shops managing to buy only a single camisole. 'I think your plan just backfired, big fellah,' Pete tells Adam, helpfully.

Now that Adam and Rachel are a confirmed if cautious couple, it's only natural that their friends should get to know each other – and so, for the first time, all three couples are in the same place at the same time, enjoying an evening at David and Karen's house. While the girls discuss motherhood in the front

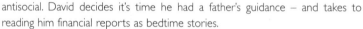

Cold Facts

⑥ Mike Bullen had just become a father for the first time when the first series was written, and many of the scenes – including the ante-natal class quiz – were drawn from life.

⑥ The prosthetic stomach that Fay Ripley wore in the birth scene cost £2000. She also had to wear a pubic wig for extra verisimilitude.

'The word "life" will no longer apply. You will simply exist to meet your child's every demand.'

Karen gives the new parents some encouragement

room, the boys sneak off to the pub and indulge in that favourite male debate – what do women want? Adam, feeling the warm glow of romance that only several pints can bring, borrows Pete's mobile to phone Rachel and ask her to move in with him. But he doesn't get the answer he expects. Why should she sacrifice everything to go and live with him? Why doesn't he come to live with her? The conversation collapses into drunken bickering, and Adam storms off with Pete's mobile in his pocket...

Jenny's time is drawing near. While Pete goes into a frenzy of preparation, Jenny succumbs to a terrible attack of pre-birth nerves – and no amount of organisation can make it better. Pete's as scared as she is, and finally, after a shouting match over the toothbrushes and pyjamas, they admit that they're terrified of the event that they've been looking forward to so single-mindedly for the last nine months.

The next day, Jenny's pottering around the flat when – ouch! – her labour begins. She follows the plan and calls Pete on his mobile – only to get through to a remorseful, hungover Adam on his way into work. There's no time for explanations; Adam races to the hospital, calling Rachel to beg her to track down Pete for him. The chase is on.

Pete, meanwhile, is undergoing torture of a different kind, learning to play golf under the overbearing tutelage of David. Suddenly a car bursts on to the golf course... Rachel's car! Pete rushes off to meet her, leaving a very confused David behind him. Rachel doesn't play golf, does she?

As Pete and Rachel negotiate the Manchester traffic, Adam is speeding across town in a taxi, trying to explain to the deeply unimpressed driver that his best friend's wife is having a baby that he knows nothing about. The cabbie, disgusted at what he takes to be moral degeneracy, refuses Adam's money.

Jenny's been wheeled into the labour room, and is in agony: so much agony, in fact, that it barely registers when she sees Adam, rather than Pete, turn up to be her birthing partner. A squeamish Adam is forced down to the business end to keep her informed on what's coming out – but he soon gets the hang of it, and before long he's cheering her on to a successful birth.

Things aren't going so well for the back-up brigade; Rachel's been stopped by a motorcycle traffic policeman, and narrowly avoids a speeding ticket. But he turns out to be a knight in shining armour and, turning on his blue lights, whisks Pete off to the hospital in the nick of time. The flustered father arrives to find Jenny, Adam... and his new son. The baby narrowly avoids being called Preston, in honour of the policeman, and ends up being named Adam Preston Gifford.

It's this drama that cements the bond between Karen and David, Adam and Rachel, Pete and Jenny. As they coo over the cradle of little Adam Preston Gifford, each of them ponders the future. Will Karen have another child? Will Adam and Rachel get their own place? And what will life be like now for Pete and Jenny, with a small baby to look after? Watch this space.

Back together again, after a long wait.

SCENE 57A INT
SET PETE & JENNY'S HOUSE - BEDROOM
NIGHT 8 2335
JENNY:PETE:

JENNY SITS ON THE BED AS PETE PACKS HER AN OVERNIGHT BAG FOR HER HOSPITAL STAY. WATCHING THESE PREPARATIONS BRINGS HOME TO HER THE IMEDIACY AND (MORE IMPORTANTLY) THE ENORMITY OF WHAT SHE'S FACING. PETE BUSIES ABOUT, TAKING CLOTHES OUT OF CUPBOARDS.

PETE: I knew this bag wasn't big enough.

JENNY: What are you doing?

PETE: Just checking.

THAT'S GOOD ENOUGH FOR PETE. HE CAREFULLY FOLDS IT ON THE BED, AVOIDING CREASES, THEN ADDS IT TO THE SUITCASE WHICH ALREADY CONTAINS KNICKERS, TOWELS, SLIPPERS ETC.

JENNY: Pete can't we just go to bed? You can do all that when my waters break.

PETE: You won't want to be bothered with it then. Now, let's see... (PETE CONSULTS THE CHECK LIST) Maternity bra?

JENNY: I'm wearing it.

PETE GIVES HER A LOOK - 'DON'T BE DIFFICULT'.

PETE: Uh, uh Madam.

JENNY: (RELUCANTLY) It's in the bag.

PETE FETCHES ONE, ADDING IT TO THE PILE OF CLOTHES, THEN AGAIN BURIES HIS HEAD IN MIRIAM

JENNY: Pete?

PETE: (WITHOUT LOOKING UP) Yeah?

JENNY: (LOOKING AT CLOTHES - FEARFULLY) Pete, I'm getting really close now.

PETE: (ABSENTLY) Hmm.

HE TAKES MORE CLOTHES FROM THE CUPBOARD AND ADDS THEM TO THE SUITCASE. JENNY GETS OFF THE BED.

JENNY: (AN EDGE TO HER VOICE) Would you stop doing that?

PETE: (OFF-HAND FAILING TO NOTICE THE EDGE IN HER VOICE) You'll thank me in the long run. (HOLDS UP TWO DRESSING GOWNS FROM THE BACK OF THE WARDROBE) Now, I thought this dressing gown. Do you really want to wear the blue one? Cos there's...

JENNY SNATCHES THE NEARER DRESSING GOWN OUT OF PETE'S HANDS, WANTING HIM TO STOP PACKING.

JENNY: No!!! Could you stop it, please!

PETE SHRUGS, AND FOLDING THE OTHER DRESSING GOWN, ADDS IT TO THE SUITCASE. JENNY RIPS IT FROM THE SUITCASE AND FLINGS IT ASIDE. A COUPLE OF PAIRS OF KNICKERS GO FLYING AS WELL.

JENNY: I'm not ready, Pete!

PETE: (RETRIEVING KNICKERS AND GOING TO RE-PACK THEM) Jen...

JENNY BEGINS TO GET A BIT BESERK. SHE RIPS THE PANTIES FROM PETE'S HANDS AND FLINGS THEM ASIDE, THEN STARTS THROWING OUT EVERYTHING HE'S PACKED INTO THE BAG. KNICKERS, NIGHTDRESSES, BREAST PADS, SANITARY TOWELS GO FLYING ACROSS THE ROOM.

JENNY: (HYSTERICALLY) You're driving me mad!

PETE: It took me ages to do all that...

JENNY: Just forget about my knickers! Forget about my nightie. Forget about my toothbrush!...

PETE: (BUTTING IN REMEMBERING) Toothbrush! I knew there was something...

JENNY: Ahhhhhhh!

PETE MAKES AS IF TO GO TO THE BATHROOM TO FETCH THE TOOTHBRUSH. HE DOESN'T EVEN MAKE IT OUT OF THE ROOM. JENNY FLINGS HIM AGAINST A WARDROBE, PINNING HIM THERE, AND STARING AT HIM, BREATHING HEAVILY, A WOMAN ON THE VBERGE... PETE LOOKS AT HER SHOCKED, AND SLIGHTLY SCARED.

PETE: (NERVOUSLY) Jen, are you all right love?

JENNY RELEASES HER HOLD ON PETE.

JENNY: Pete. You don't understand!

A BEAT; NO HE DOESN'T.

JENNY: I'm scared shitless. I'm going to have a baby.

PETE DOESN'T KNOW WHAT TO DO.

PETE: (LIMPLY) I know. (BEAT, LAMELY) I don't know what to do.

JENNY: (IMPLORINGLY) Just give us a hug.

HE TAKES HER IN HIS ARMS AND HUGS HER. ALL THE FEAR THAT'S BEEN WELLING UP INSIDE JENNY BURSTS FORTH. SHE SOBS IN HIS ARMS. HE HUGS HER TIGHTLY. THEY CLING TO EACH OTHER FOR DEAR LIFE.

Episode 2

Rachel reveals that she's married — and, more to the point, has never got divorced ... Pete and Jenny find it hard to adjust to parenthood ... and David's lost £15,000 in dodgy investments

Adam and Rachel have finally decided to bite the bullet and move in together – not into one of their flats, but into a new rented flat in Didsbury, where they can begin a new life. As they sit in the cluttered living room on their first night together, surrounded by cardboard boxes containing a lifetime's worth of Rachel's memorabilia, Adam discovers what he takes at first to be a fake wedding certificate. But there's nothing fake about it, as Rachel unwillingly confesses: she really did get married, many years ago, to a man called Kris Bumstead. It didn't last (he ran off with her best friend)... but they didn't get divorced either. This comes as a bombshell to Adam, who storms out of the house and pitches up on Pete and Jenny's doorstep, a broken man.

Pete and Jenny, however, are having problems of their own. Their joy as new parents was short-lived, and now they're living out a nightmare of sleeplessness, short tempers and dirty nappies. Pete's so exhausted he's falling asleep on old ladies' shoulders on the tram into work; Jenny's anxious about motherhood, terrified of doing something wrong and drowning in an unfamiliar sea of baby products. It's hard to keep the relationship sweet when, every time they crawl exhuasted into bed, the baby starts crying again. So the last thing they need is Adam coming to stay with them. Despite his best intentions, he turns out to be the houseguest from hell. A well-meaning offer to babysit nearly turns into disaster when he attempts to demonstrate the baby's survival instincts by hanging it on the clothesline... luckily, a basket of washing provides a soft landing.

The Ballad of Rachel Bradley
by Adam Williams

There was a girl called Rachel Bradley
Whose boyfriend loved her truly, deeply, madly
She was married to Kris with a K
But now that bollocks with a B has gone away
So Rachel's now a divorcee
Living with Adam in Didsbury
And Kris with a K, he's now her ex
So Rachel with an R, can we have some...

Pete and Jenny discover that parenthood
is not all it's cracked up to be.

Pete and Jenny discover that parenthood is not all it's cracked up to be.

Things are no better at David and Karen's, where Rachel runs for comfort. David's discovered that one of his investments (a golf-course in a small African state) isn't going to be quite as profitable as he'd imagined; in fact, he's lost £15,000. No skiing holidays for Karen this year, then; even a week in the Lake District seems to be beyond their budget. And suddenly David, who was so keen on Karen having another baby, thinks it might be a good idea for her to go back on the pill.

Persuaded that it would be a good idea to contact her husband with a view to getting a divorce, Rachel arranges to meet Kris in a Manchester restaurant. She's prepared to be ruthless – but as soon as he walks in, all her good intentions go out the window. She still fancies Kris just as much as she ever did, and before the meal is over they're reminiscing about the old days and entering into dangerously flirtatious territory. Kris sees her home and ends up staying the night... and the word 'divorce' has never been mentioned.

Things are getting very fraught at Pete and Jenny's. The baby won't stop crying, they're bickering constantly and having Adam there is just making matters worse. Finally, after one smart remark too many, Adam's back on the street with his bag in his hand, and he has no option but to swallow his pride and go home to Rachel, married or not. But he's greeted at the door by an unexpected sight: a topless Kris claiming that Rachel's been sick down his shirt.

And so begins a domestic war of attrition. Adam can't win. Kris is a DIY genius (he fixes the long-malfunctioning toilet), a great cook (roast turkey beats microwave lasagne), a talented musician and unreasonably fit and attractive. Adam's only option is to play Tammy Wynette's D.I.V.O.R.C.E. at earspllitting volume, and to retreat to the golf course and whack a few balls around the place. Rachel's girlfriends, aware of the agony that Adam's going through, take her to one side and tell her, in no uncertain terms, to make her choice.

And so Rachel, in a rare moment of clarity, gives Kris a cheque for £500 to help him on his way, and asks him, ever so sweetly, for a divorce. He agrees; it's as simple as that. Adam, unaware of all this, charges in waving his money about, gives Kris £500 just to get out of town, and considers it money well spent. Kris, with £1000 in his pocket, heads back to London, leaving Adam and Rachel alone and happy (even if they can no longer afford a sofa to sit on).

Thanks to some astute money management by Karen, who has taken over the financial reins from David, £1000 drops out of the sky only to land, in the shape of a handsome leather sofa, in Adam and Rachel's flat. And so, as Adam serenades Rachel on an out-of-tune guitar, they begin their lives together at last.

Episode 3

An unintentional game of Chinese whispers causes havoc in the bedrooms of Manchester. In this episode, a merry-go-round of sexual dysfunction and misunderstandings.

Karen's feeling romantic, but David just wants to play FTSE.

It all starts off with David, who's under a lot of pressure at work and is finding it difficult to perform in bed with Karen. She's very understanding, tells him that it happens to all men at some time or another, and that he shouldn't worry. But David's not the sort of man to take something like that lying down, and so he decides to ask a friend for advice. He chooses Adam. This turns out to be a very large mistake.

Adam is having no such problems; he and Rachel are at it hammer and tongs at every available opportunity. So when David tells him, over a game of squash, that he's having difficulty getting it up, Adam's response is to make light of it. But David's serious, and so Adam promises to ask around a few male friends and see if he can come up with any practical advice.

Male friends, in Adam's case, means Pete. And so, over a pint at the pub, Adam sketches out the case of 'a friend of mine' who has a 'temporary bout of impotence'. He's trying to spare David's feelings by naming no names – but Pete jumps to the obvious conclusion: it's Adam who's having the problem, not this imaginary 'friend'.

Pete's up for it, but Jenny just wants a decent night's sleep.

Pete finds it comforting to know that his cocksure friend isn't all he's cracked up to be — because he, too, is on short rations in the bedroom. It's only a month since baby Adam was born, and Jenny's far from ready to resume sexual relations. It looks like there's another six weeks to go before Pete can look forward to his conjugal rights — so, to while away the time, he tells Jenny that they're not the only ones who aren't getting regular sex. And so the rumour spreads...

After that, there's no stopping it. Jenny, on a shopping trip with Karen, mentions that Adam and Rachel are no longer satisfying each other. Karen passes this information on to David, who is hugely encouraged to learn that arrogant Adam, who treated his problem so lightly, is in the same boat as him. Buoyed up by this piece of information, he leaps on top of his wife, only to discover that his own impotence, the source of all this mischief, is still very much in evidence.

It soon becomes apparent that David's problems stem from a stressful work situation. His colleague, the dreadful Natalie, bullies him over a proposed merger, their conversation fraught with double entendres ('You're not going soft on me, are you? There's no room in this company for limp dicks...'). And so David, furious, decides to take it all out on Adam. They line up another squash game, during which David drops the bombshell: Rachel has been going around telling everyone that she's not satisfied in bed. Adam's game collapses as he begins to think the unthinkable: that he, Adam Williams, stud-about-town, is not all he's cracked up to be...

Desperate times call for desperate measures, and our sexually confused heroes embark on a varied course of remedies. For Rachel, who's heard from Karen that Adam's losing interest in her, that means going to an underwear shop and buying some sexy lingerie. For Adam, that means a trip to the local sex store, where a contemptuous shop assistant directs him to the straight sex manuals 'just beyond necrophilia'. Pete, meanwhile, races off into the night to find a packet of condoms; his big night has arrived, only for Jenny to announce that she's refusing to play unless he takes responsibility for contraception. Finally they realise that parenthood has changed their relationship; they're no longer kids with no responsibilities, but they can continue to make love as adults, as parents, for the rest of their lives.

S.Ė.x

♡ Fay Ripley wrote most of the scene in which she fantasises about being a Victorian maid herself (Mike Bullen's original version involved a Sumo wrestler)

♡ The scene in which Rachel and Adam have sex in a shop window was inspired by one of Mike Bullen's real-life girlfriends (although she never actually persuaded him to do it).

David, typically, takes the most extreme path, deciding that the only person who can cure him of his impotence is a 'professional' – who, in this case, is a nice young prostitute called Trixie. She's seen them all before, the stressed-out professionals who just want to talk, and tells him, with a large dollop of worldly wisdom, that he's got to get on top of his job before he gets on top of his wife. David leaves, his virtue still intact, to put these wise words into practice. The next day at work he's a changed man, confronting Natalie, solving problems and generally acting like the cock of the walk – much to Karen's delight.

Adam and Rachel have revved themselves up into such a state that neither is sure whether they're really enjoying sex or not. The lingerie seems to have worked, and Adam's picked up a few tips from his manual; in particular, he's focusing on the idea that their love life should be more adventurous. Eventually he forces Rachel to confess that her one great fantasy is to make love in a shop window – although possibly a Manchester branch of Oxfam was not exactly what she had in mind. But that's the best Adam can offer, and, such is his devotion to the cause, he borrows the shop keys and leads his baffled partner to a large double bed that's been set up in the display window.

All seems to be going well when the lovers hear the click of a lock; they're shut into the shop for the night. It could be worse; they'll just have to keep themselves busy till morning. And then, out of nowhere, a car crashes through the window, joyriders scatter in all directions and Adam and Rachel find themselves taken into custody. Fortunately for them, the arresting officer is none other than Adam's old friend Preston, who was present at the birth of Jenny's baby, and he lets them off with a caution. Adam and Rachel realise that they've been the victims of a misunderstanding, and return home to make things up in the best possible way.

Unlike their friends, Adam and Rachel can't get enough.

Episode 4

Will Karen have an affair with her charming new author? ...
Will Adam rediscover his long-dormant literary talent? ...
And can Pete and his father stop arguing for five minutes?

Now that Josh is a year old and has Ramona to look after him, Karen has gone back to work – and she's finding it hard to juggle her working life with her domestic routine. As a result, David's living off takeaways (although it hasn't occurred to him that he might cook) and Karen barely has time for her old friends. So she's less than enthusiastic when her boss pulls her off the children's book she's been struggling through and asks her to edit the new novel by Alexander Welch. Alexander Welch! The author of *Blanket of Tears*, the most erotic novel Karen has ever read! That scene where she's ironing...! All her girlfriends are duly impressed (Rachel admits 'I read it with one hand'), but Karen's not sure; she's finding work hard enough already, without the extra stress of a celebrity author and a high-profile publication.

Karen and Alec find themselves working very closely
together!

Alexander Welch, or Alec to his friends (and everyone's his friend) takes matters into his own hands, turns up uninvited at David and Karen's one weekend, charms their guests and soon has Karen eating out of his hand. He's persuasive all right – and Karen agrees to edit his new novel.

Inspired by this brush with literary fame, Adam decides that he, too, could be a writer. This is the answer to all his prayers! Only the other night he'd been complaining to Pete in the pub that life seemed to have passed him by, that he's hurtling towards middle age with nothing to show for it but a job he's not interested in and a domestic routine that's comfortable, no longer exciting. Of course: he'll become a writer! He tried once and 'it was shite', but Alec assured him that 'first drafts are always shite' – and so, glowing with inspiration, Adam roots around in the attic until he finds that precious literary fragment: *Trainspotting* by Adam Williams ('I knew that was a good title'). But Adam was right first time: it is shite. 'Night. Winter. Dark. Cold. The howl of a dog, an anthem of despair,' it begins, and that's the best bit. Even Adam has to admit that *Trainspotting* might not be his best bet – but he's not going to give up on his

Three generations of Giffords.

dreams of becoming a writer just like that. Not when there's a wonderful story developing right under his nose...

Pete has never got on well with his father; they're too alike, too pedantic, they argue constantly about trivial things ('A34? What's wrong with the M6?') and never

seem able to tell each other how they really feel. So a visit from Pete's parents is a form of torture for the young parents. Pete's Mum sees herself as a domestic goddess, hoovering around people, washing clean plates ('they gather dust in the cupboard') and poking her nose in where it's not wanted. You might think that a new grandson would calm them down a bit, but not a bit of it: Pete and his father find themselves arguing over the child's cot. 'I'm going to be a good Dad to him,' says Pete. 'I wanted to be to you,' says his Dad, in a rare moment of candour. 'Yeah, well, we can't have everything...' says Pete – and the moment is gone.

Karen's quickly discovering that life as a high-flying editor has its compensations. Alec Welch is an accomplished flirt, and, over one of their long 'working' lunches, he not only tells Karen that he's going to dedicate the book to her, but he also touches her – twice! Karen relates this with breathless excitement to Rachel, who's alarmed to see her friend plunging headlong into an affair, albeit with a famous writer. 'So adultery's fine as long as it's with a celebrity?' asks Rachel (who really ought to know better). But Karen doesn't care; she's caught up in the romance of it all, and she thinks that Alec is really keen on her. Ramona overhears her on the phone to Alec, and immediately jumps to conclusions. In a panic, Ramona phones David and begs him to come home, quoting some of the things she's heard; David, somewhat flattered, believes that Ramona is declaring her passion for him.

The book launch approaches, and Alec's off to Liverpool to do a reading – accompanied by his lovely editor. Karen thinks this is it: away from home, in a hotel, flushed by success, the inevitable will happen. And so, that night, she taps on Alec's bedroom door, a bottle of champagne in her hand, to toast 'their' success. The stage is set for a great seduction – until it quickly becomes apparent that Alec has other plans. A young blonde woman emerges from the bathroom, Alec offers Karen a puff on his joint – and she flees back to Manchester.

David, meanwhile, has 'discovered', thanks to the big mouth of Adam Williams, that Karen is almost certainly having an affair with Alec. Furious that he's being cuckolded by a man he believed (mistakenly) to be his friend, David races home

Adam discovers that sometimes you have to suffer for your art!

to get his revenge ('Well, two can play at that game!') by sleeping with Ramona.

Drunk and amorous, he creeps upstairs to the nanny's room, ignoring a note that's been left for him at the bottom of the stairs. Mumbling sweet nothings in Spanish, he climbs into bed beside a slumbering woman... his wife! She's sleeping in the nanny's bed because Josh has a cold and she wants to be near him. It doesn't take Karen long to put two and two together and realise that David was trying it on with Ramona – and that, somehow, it's Adam's fault.

Adam, however, is far too busy to care about such things. He's going to be a writer. His new novel, *Like Father, Like Son*, will make his name – well, once he's got around to changing a few details, like the names. Perhaps it wasn't such a good idea to call the central character 'Pete' ('Pete was never a slave to fashion, and his style was as flexible as his girth'). And perhaps it wasn't a good idea to leave the manuscript lying around where Pete could find it. Pete and Adam have a huge falling out – just in time for baby Adam's christening, at which his namesake was to have been godfather. It's up to Jenny to act as peacemaker and persuade Adam to destroy the manuscript.

Adam does so willingly – but only after he's been told, in no uncertain terms, that it's unpublishable shite of the worst kind. That's Karen's verdict – and it's a neat way of getting her own back on Adam for telling David about her interest in Alexander Welch.

Pete and Jo's wedding was a slice of heaven. Beautiful weather, a beautiful beach...

...and a beautiful ceremony.
But Jo didn't learn from David and Karen's experience... and paid the price.

David, Karen and Mark could have told her that affairs cause nothing but heartache and can lead to violence.

On a happier note, Adam discovered that a rose up the bum is worth more than a dozen in the hand. He got the girl...

Consequences

And a baby.

Jenny's limo fantasy became a reality. But she found out the hard way that reality rarely lives up to the dream.

Gambling and pole dancing are not great
ways to get more money – particularly if
your employer catches you doing the latter.

But for all their ups and downs, the friendships have remained strong, sometimes a little battered, but then time heals most things...

The day of the christening arrives. Pete and Adam are friends again, but Pete's fallen out with his father over the question of the baby's name. For generations, the name 'Algernon' has gone down the Gifford line, but Pete (who was called 'Algy', 'Algae' and 'Pond Scum' at school) is determined that it will end with baby Adam. And so the christening goes ahead without the grandparents. Jenny's scary Christian sister reads some entirely unsuitable texts about hellfire, then Adam gets up to read out a letter from Pete's father. 'I know that Pete will be a good father,' it reads. 'I've seen the way he looks at his son. With love. A love that only a father can recognise. And which I recognise because it's how I look at Pete.'

And then Pete's mobile phone rings. It's his Mum. Pete's father dropped dead of a heart attack on his way to the church.

And so the christening is followed by a funeral. The gravestone reads 'Algernon Edward Gifford, father of Peter Algernon, grandfather of Adam Preston Algernon'.

Jenny and Adam Preston Algernon

Episode 5

Karen and David try marriage guidance ... Jenny and Rachel are desperate for some time to themselves ... While Pete and Adam hit the Manchester clubs looking for thrills

Is middle age catching up with our heroes? Jenny admits that all she and Pete do these days is 'eat crap and watch TV. Very much like being in an old people's home'. Rachel finds that, now the first flush of romance has worn off, she's getting more and more irritated by Adam's personal habits: catching peanuts in his mouth, using the toilet while she's brushing her teeth, munching popcorn all the way through her favourite Ingmar Bergman movie, that sort of thing. And as for David and Karen – they're going into marriage guidance (reluctantly, on David's part). Clearly something has to be done to bring the spark back into three ailing relationships.

The girls

Pete's idea of the ideal present, the very thing that will put the sparkle back into his marriage, is to subscribe to cable TV ('it's the choice!'). Jenny has other ideas; she's determined to get out of the house once in a while, and manages to secure Rachel's services as a babysitter. Rachel's delighted; it will get her away from Adam for an evening. But things don't work out quite as planned. Pete and Jenny find themselves sitting in an Indian restaurant with nothing to talk about other than the baby. Rachel can't shake Adam off that easily; lured by Pete's cable TV, he suddenly decides that babysitting can be quite good fun, especially as it allows him to talk all the way through

Blast from the Past

👁 A brief flashback scene, in which we see Pete and Adam as kids playing football, took a whole day to film. The children, who were chosen to look like the adult actors, wore late-70s-style wigs. James Nesbitt didn't see the resemblance to his 'mini-me' until the boy showed that he could raise one eyebrow, in spot-on Nesbitt style.

episodes of *The Sweeney* and *Charlie's Angels*. Rachel goes off in a huff and leaves him to it – and by the time Adam gets home, Rachel's well and truly stoned, thanks to her next-door-neighbour Emma, an attractive 18-year-old with a ready supply of dope. Adam's indignation is quickly tempered; he's fancied Emma for ages, ever since Rachel started going out jogging with her, and he imagines that he's in with a chance. This fantasy is rapidly dashed, however: Emma confesses that if she spotted Adam in a club she'd assume that he'd come to pick up his daughter. Rachel, somewhat the worse for wear, loses her temper with Adam and ends up hitting him. Twice.

Karen and David's first session of couples therapy doesn't go too well. David's only there because Adam's convinced him that it's a good idea to go and fight his corner – and when he discovers that the counsellor is a woman, and a divorced woman at that, he does everything he can to undermine her. This includes listening to his radio, setting off alarms and being generally obnoxious in the way only David Marsden can be – but, ultimately, the counsellor manages to persuade him that there's work to be done. David agrees to a fresh start: he and Karen will go out on a 'date' and try to discover what made their relationship tick in the first place. Karen remembers their first meeting: David rescued her from the unwanted attentions of a drunken groper with the deathless line 'Can I be of any assistance?'. Warmed by the memory, they look forward to their first date.

Pete and Adam go clubbing – two fish
out of water!

'Let's let our hair down.
While we still have some.'

Karen, as a 'single' woman, suddenly seems very attractive to David: not least because he sees her being chatted up by an equally attractive single man. After a rather awkward start, their date goes well, and they head off home with stars in their eyes.

Still attempting to recapture the rapture of youth, Adam and Pete organise what they hope will be a big night out (and, under duress, they take David along with them). It starts off as a pub crawl – but Manchester pubs appear to be dead on that particular night, and Pete would much rather stay in the Nag's Head anyway. Adam has other plans. 'Let's let our hair down while we still have some!', he insists, and leads them off to a warehouse club with the famous last words 'Trust me: I'm Irish'. David's turned away at the door, much to his relief; Adam and Pete get in (only just, as Adam has already tried to buy drugs off the doorman) and set about getting 'sorted' with grim determination.

The girls, meanwhile, have gone to a party, where they quickly discover that life as a single girl isn't as much fun as they remember. Jenny gets quickly drunk and starts leaping on any passing man. Rachel gets chatted up by a very boring accountant, only to be rescued by an equally uninspiring solicitor. Karen, meanwhile, runs into Neil – the very man who attempted to chat her up before her date with David – and finds herself in an unwanted clinch on the dancefloor. Things are starting to get ugly, she's having to fight Neil off – when, suddenly, a familiar voice says 'Can I be of any assistance?'.

Adam and Pete are at large in 'the land of E', desperately trying to find some decent gear but ending up with sugar-coated sweeties instead. Adam catches sight of Emma with her boyfriend and a sleazy individual who, it transpires, is a real live drug dealer. Just as the police raid the club, the dealer thrusts a bag containing 140 ecstasy tablets into Pete's hand while Adam scraps with Emma's boyfriend on the floor. Pete and Adam – the big-time dealer and his 'muscle', according to the police – are taken into custody. An emergency call to Rachel's mobile sends a solicitor hotfooting it to the station; unfortunately for Pete and Adam, it's the solicitor from the party, who's legal experience doesn't extend much beyond conveyancing.

All is resolved when Emma tells the police what really happened, and our two fun-loving criminals are released with a pat on the back from the desk sergeant, who imagines they're drug-busting vigilantes. The lovers are reunited, and even Adam admits that, perhaps, it's better to act his age after all .

Episode 6

The six friends are off to the ball... Can they be trusted to
behave themselves? Rachel's pregnant. Adam proposes. But
a happy ending seems unlikely.

Don't be fooled by Jenny's civilised appearance.

David has invited his friends to a big
charity ball – the sort of thing where
you pay £50 for a ticket and have to
wear evening dress. Adam loves it:
there's free champagne (which, to his
astonishment, Rachel isn't drinking)
and he can pretend to be James Bond.
Pete and Jenny feel awkward and
intimidated, and Jenny reacts by taking
a bit more fizz than is good for her.
And so, when she finds herself on a
table with David's dreadful colleague
Natalie, it's only a matter of time
before she loses her temper. That's not
difficult with the dreadful Natalie, who
chips away at Jenny until she can bear
no more and does what any woman
would do under the circumstances:
she lets off a fire extinguisher all over
her tormentor's dress.

That's not the only surprise of the evening. Karen corners Rachel in the toilet,
where she's spent most of the evening, and extracts a confession from her: she's
pregnant. And it might not be Adam's baby. Gradually, as mayhem is breaking out
in the main hall, the whole story comes out. On that drunken first night with her
ex-husband, when she was sick over his top and Adam came home
unexpectedly, Rachel and Kris had sex. 'Didn't you take any precautions?' asks a
horrified Karen. 'Well,' says Rachel, 'I locked the front door...' And so there's not
telling whose the baby is. Karen advises an appointment with the gynaecologist,
who will be able to pinpoint the date of conception and thus remove any
uncertainty.

Rachel's already suffering from morning sickness, but spins a yarn to Adam about some dodgy mussels she ate at the weekend, and promises to see a doctor for a check-up. Adam, being a supportive boyfriend, goes along to hold her hand at the hospital, only to discover that Rachel's not in casualty, where he expected to see her, but in a different department altogether, having her insides scanned. 'Is it a kidney stone?' he asks, baffled by the image on the screen... And then the penny drops. Adam's not sure how to respond; he's never thought of himself as a father, even though he feels that the time is right for him and Rachel to get married. But a baby? Is this something that either of them really wants?

Adam stalks off to think things over, and meets a young woman breastfeeding her child in the town square. At first she's hostile ('If you want to stare at tits, why don't you buy *Playboy*?') but, when she understands Adam's predicament, she turns friendly. Too friendly for her thug of a boyfriend, it turns out, who arrives on the bus and promptly socks Adam in the eye for being too pally with his missus.

Adam pops the question with his usual style.

This seems to be enough to make Adam's mind up, and the next night he takes Rachel out for dinner in a posh restaurant. It's a pleasant evening, but both are distracted, preoccupied; she's desperately worried about her pregnancy, and he's got something else on his mind. Finally, over coffee, he pulls off a typical Adam Williams production number: he snaps his fingers and the waiters wheel on a huge cake, decorated with little bridal figurines and a stork carrying a baby; Adam drops down on one knee and offers Rachel a ring. Rachel's stunned, and bursts into tears – tears of joy, Adam assumes, as the rest of the diners gather round to offer their congratulations. But when Rachel's still crying some minutes later, Adam realises something is wrong – and that's when he learns that the baby may not be his.

Adam takes refuge with Jenny; Pete's out somewhere, they've had a row. Jenny is kind and understanding – and then, to the surprise of both, their friendly comfort session turns into a long, passionate kiss. They spring apart, embarrassed and confused, just as Pete arrives home. What, wonders Adam, is going on here? If Rachel's screwing her ex-husband, and his first response is to kiss his best friend's wife, are they really cut out for a life together?

David, meanwhile, is coping with the fall-out from the fire extinguisher incident. Natalie is on the warpath; 'ordinarily I'd sue Jenny's ass off, but then this isn't the States... unfortunately'. She demands not only a cheque to cover her

Sometimes the line between friendship and love becomes blurred for Jenny and Adam.

ruined dress, but also a grovelling letter of apology. That's a step too far for Jenny. Fair enough, she'll pay for the dress, but she's not sorry for what she did and she won't say she is. It's an awkward situation – for all her faults, Natalie is still David's superior, and he can't just tell her to sling her hook. Fortunately for (nearly) all concerned, David discovers that Natalie's

job is on the line, and that he's the only person who can save her – on condition, of course, that she agrees to forget about the fire extinguisher. 'You're such a bullshitter!' says Karen, full of admiration. 'It's what they pay me for,' replies a self-satisfied David.

Adam's in a daze. His world has fallen apart. He's split up with Rachel, he's not going to be a father – or, at least, if he is going to be a father he can't be sure if the child is really his. How can he decide what to do? A chance meeting with the young mother and her pugilistic partner persuades him that, after all, he really loves Rachel despite all her faults, and that he should be prepared to stand by her through this crisis. Rachel, however, has other ideas. She can't stand the uncertainty; she loves Adam, who doesn't want to know, while Kris is offering to stand as father to a child that may or may not be his. Beaten down by doubt, she invites her friends around and drops the bombshell: she's leaving Manchester to go and stay with her sister in London until the baby's born.

Adam, on learning the news, races to the railway station for what he hopes will be a romantic reunion and a happy ending. The reality, however, is far from the fantasy. Rachel's already on the train at Piccadilly, determined to leave for good, and despite Adam's protestations she knows in her heart that he could never really trust her until the baby's born. And that kind of doubt is something she could never stand...

The train pulls out of Piccadilly, leaving a broken Adam to be led home by his old friends Pete and Jenny.

SCENE 79
Int PICCADILLY STATION
Day 7 1910

ADAM: RACHEL: RAILWAY GUARD:

ADAM RUNS DOWN THE PLATFORM, LOOKING IN WINDOWS FOR RACHEL. NO
MUSIC A LA BRIEF ENCOUNTER ACCOMPANIES HIM, RATHER AN ADENOIDAL
RAILTRACK ANNOUNCEMENT OVER THE TANNOY, ANNOUNCING A DELAY TO A
PARTICULAR TRAIN (NOT THE LONDON ONE).

ADAM: (CALLING) Rachel! Rachel!

RACHEL: (NOT EXCITED, BUT SURPRISED) Adam?

ADAM RUSHES UP TO HER

ADAM: Rachel! Don't go. Stay! I don't care whose baby it is. I'll
be its father.

RACHEL: (SADLY) I wanted to go without seeing you.

ADAM: (A BIT TAKEN ABACK BY THIS) What? Why?

RACHEL: Because I (NEARLY SAYS 'LOVE YOU')... because I hate
myself, Adam. I've ruined everything. It could never be the same
between us again.

ADAM: I love you! Enough for both of us!

RACHEL: Enough for three?

ADAM: Yes! Even if it's his.

RACHEL: You can't say that.

ADAM: I can! I just did.

RACHEL: Well you can't mean it.

ADAM: I do! I did! (WORRIED THE TRAIN MIGHT BE ABOUT TO GO, ADAM
PULLS OPEN RACHEL'S DOOR) Rachel, please! You've got to get off
this train.

RACHEL: (NOT GETTING OFF) Adam... It is his.

THAT PULLS ADAM UP SHORT. HE'S SPEECHLESS A BEAT.

ADAM: (FLATLY) Is it?

RACHEL: You see. You want to mean it. But you can't until you know for sure.

ADAM: Is it his?

RACHEL: (GETTING OFF THE TRAIN BUT LEAVING HER BAGS ON) I don't know. But that's the whole point, isn't it? Every day that I'm pregnant we'll be wondering. And dreading the moment of truth. I can't go through that, Adam. For the baby's sake.

RAILWAY GUARD: (SHOUTING DOWN THE PLATFORM) You're going to have to close the door now.

RACHEL CLIMBS ONTO THE TRAIN, LEAVING THE DOOR OPEN, AND LOOKS AT ADAM, WONDERING IF HE UNDERSTANDS. A BEAT, THEN ADAM CLOSES THE DOOR. RACHEL LEANS DOWN AND THEY KISS. THE TRAIN STARTS MOVING, TEARING THEIR LIPS APART. ADAM WATCHES AS THE TRAIN GATHERS SPEED. HE DOESN'T WAVE, AND NEITHER DOES RACHEL. THEY JUST WATCH THE DISTANCE GROWING BETWEEN THEM.

THE TRAIN EXITS THE STATION AND DISAPPEARS FROM VIEW. ADAM STANDS, WATCHING THE SPACE WHERE THE TRAIN HAD BEEN. FINALLY, HE TURNS... TO FIND JENNY AND PETE WALKING TOWARDS HIM. HE LOOKS AT THEM IN SHOCK.

ADAM: She's gone.

JENNY NODS SADLY - SHE THOUGHT SHE MIGHT.

PETE: Come on, mate. Let's go home.

ADAM NODS - THERE'S NOTHING ELSE TO DO. WITH ADAM IN THE MIDDLE AND WITH PETE AND JENNY'S ARMS AROUND HIM, THEY WALK AWAY.

FREEZE FRAME OR FADE TO BLACK.

<u>END OF EPISODE SIX</u>

Christine Langan and Andy Harries

(PRODUCER AND EXECUTIVE PRODUCER)

As with all births, **Cold Feet** wasn't produced by just one person. Mike Bullen was the writer and creator of the show, but it's unlikely that there would have been a **Cold Feet** at all without producer Christine Langan and executive producer Andy Harries, who brought Bullen's ideas to the screen and saw the show through its first few years.

The relationship began in 1995 when Bullen's agent sent a script to Andy Harries, then head of comedy at Granada. Harries had started the comedy department in 1992, and was looking for new material that would reflect the life of his peer group – upwardly mobile people in their 30s, a demographic he felt was under-served at the time. Bullen's script, a play about an FA Cup final called *My Perfect Match*, was fresh,

> **'I loved it right away and put it straight into production.'**
> ANDY HARRIES

funny and contemporary. 'I loved it right away,' says Harries, 'and put it straight into production. The dialogue seemed to capture the way that people of my age lived their lives. It sounds strange to say this now, but there was really nothing on TV in the mid 90s that showed that. My

generation wasn't exactly a lost generation, but there was nothing on TV that reflected our lives. Mike was the first writer who tapped into that.'

My Perfect Match was filmed with Con O'Neill and Saskia Reeves in the leads (and John Thomson in a minor role); Christine Langan, then a script editor at Granada, came on as assistant producer. It was a good team, and Harries was keen to get more material out of them. 'I wanted Mike to do a series, and so I sent him and Christine off to pick up ideas. All three of us were very much encouraged by American television like *Thirtysomething* and *Friends*, shows which tapped into the zeitgeist of our generation and seemed fresh and charming. We wanted something of the same quality for British audiences.'

'Our touchstone was always *When Harry Met Sally*,' says Christine Langan. 'It encapsulated that American way of doing comedy drama, of telling a story that could be funny but also dramatic, in which the two things were not ghettoised. That

Andy
Harries

**'We wanted
something of the
same quality for
British audiences.'**
ANDY HARRIES

seemed to be the most appropriate way of addressing our lives. We talked a lot about ourselves, and about our friends, and there was always that mixture of funny and sad, of interesting, successful people who couldn't sort out their personal lives. There was a big gap in the market for material that addressed that kind of life, and we just dived in. There was so much material, and we became obsessed by analysing our own lives and our friends' lives.'

Bullen and Langan came up with a treatment that contained the germ of

Cold Feet. It concerned a man and a woman (Adam and Rachel,), it told the story of their relationship from both points of view and it was set in

'There was so much material, and we became obsessed by analysing our own lives and our friends' lives.'

CHRISTINE LANGAN

London. The writing provided such a broad range of domestic and romantic entanglements with Adam's friends Pete and Jenny and Rachel's friends Karen and David, each at different stages in their relationships that, with Adam and Rachel as the young, romantic heart of the narrative, Harries foresaw a long-running series and was determined to get a commission from Granada. So Langan decided that the action should relocate to Manchester – home of Granada Television.

'Once we'd got the script for the pilot, it was quite easy to get a commission,' says Harries, 'The ITV network was keen to see some new material and they said "Oh, Andy's got a project, let him do it!". They weren't worried about big casting, they said "Cast whoever you like!". I don't think

they took it seriously, to them, it was just another pilot.'

With the commission in place, the casting began. 'I'd fallen in love with John Thomson when we did *My Perfect Match*,' says Langan. 'He was quite well known around Manchester as a comedian; he'd worked with Steve Coogan and Caroline Aherne. But nobody had really seen him act before. He was so good in *My Perfect Match* that I begged Mike to write a part for him. So John was in place as Pete long before anyone else. Next we had to find a director. I saw a lot of people, then I went to meet Declan Lowney, who, at the time, was making *Father Ted*. I talked to him in the green room after they'd taped a show. He'd already read the script, and he said 'It's *The Big Chill*, basically, isn't it?'. He understood what we were getting at, and I knew he'd bring a sense of comedy and energy to the show. And it was through Declan that we found Jimmy Nesbitt. I'd loved him in *Hear My Song* and *Go Now*, and it was very refreshing to use an actor that wasn't English.'

After that, Langan handed over to casting director Kate Rhodes James, who quickly discovered that Helen Baxendale – something of a star thanks to medical series *Cardiac Arrest* – was looking for a job. 'Helen was a very big fish for us,' says Langan, 'and she was ideal for *Cold Feet*. She's

Christine
Langan

gorgeous, but slightly off-the-wall. So that was an easy piece of casting. Jenny, however, proved to be much harder. We saw a lot of actresses who came across as too hectoring and nagging; we wanted to make Jenny sympathetic. When we saw Fay Ripley, she had a left-field interpretation of the part that made Jenny spikey but loveable.

'Casting David and Karen was more trial and error. I was interested in Robert Bathurst because I associated him with sitcoms, and I liked that very disciplined comic energy. I thought it would be useful to have that kind of experience in the cast, that unashamed love of a gag. As for Hermione Norris, she was the only actress we found who made Karen into a three-dimensional character. Karen could easily be a stereotypical posh girl, but Hermione made her sexy and likeable, and she had a great rapport with Robert.'

The pilot was made and screened, and its future seemed uncertain. Harries, Langan and Bullen were always gunning for a series, but ITV didn't seem so certain. Then along came the Golden Rose of Montreux and changed all that. A commission was eventually secured and the first series went out at 10 o'clock on a Sunday night. 'It wasn't the ideal time slot,' says Harries, 'but the show held its audience well and we managed to convince the network to put the second series out at 9.30pm. It was a hell of a battle. The advertisers needed a lot of convincing, they felt that the audience wasn't good for

'We had no grand plan, other than a determination to get the series on air.'

ANDY HARRIES

them. But fortunately word of mouth did the job for us, and audiences increased a lot in that second series. We were very lucky with our cast: there was someone for everyone to identify with, whether it was the handsome one, the fat one, the posh one or whatever. We didn't design it like that; a big element of luck came in.

We had no grand plan, other than a determination to get the series on air.'

By the end of the second series, it was apparent to everyone that *Cold*

'We just told the truth about those important things like marriage and jobs for our generation.'

ANDY HARRIES

Feet was a very big hit indeed. Newspapers and magazines were taking notice, the actors were becoming stars in their own right. So what was it, exactly, that made *Cold Feet* a success? 'It's easy to say in hindsight,' says Harries, 'but we tapped into a post-Thatcher zeitgeist before anyone else. In the late 90s there was a massive, newly-affluent, young middle class that had never been seen on TV before. They weren't kids; they were over their 20s, they weren't just messing about any more, they were confronting reality, getting married, having kids, holding down jobs. We just told the truth about those important things like marriage and jobs for our generation.'

'*Cold Feet* changed our attitudes to what's worthy of focus on TV,' says Langan. 'My tagline for the show was always that we took ordinary lives and treated them as extraordinary; we endowed ordinary experience with a new prominence. That struck a chord with a lot of people. 'Wow, that's happened to someone else as well!' Our characters were just regular people, not distinguished by their careers or by crime. We were just truthful about life as it was lived at the time. We captured a vibe. *Red* magazine started talking about 'middle youth', and they cited *Cold Feet* as the perfect example of that. We also started to get slagged off by a lot of columnists like Tony Parsons and Germaine Greer, who said that

'..we took ordinary lives and treated them as extraordinary.'

CHRISTINE LANGAN

Cold Feet looked as if it had been designed by a marketing department. That really hurt, but it's true that we hit on a demographic of post-baby boom middle youth that hadn't been shown on TV before. Now it's a platitude, but back then it was new.'

Another secret of *Cold Feet*'s success was the attention to style and detail. It was always important to the producers that the show should look good, that it should have an aspirational gloss that was missing in British TV. It was shot on film, the locations were always lit to look gorgeous, and there was a consistent effort to get the most out of every shot. 'We tried very hard at the start to tickle every shot,' says Christine Langan. 'Instead of just having Adam getting up quickly from a chair when Rachel rings him, we'd put in a shot of the chair spinning around really fast – little touches like that made it more like a cartoon or a slapstick movie.' And, of course, a great deal of attention was paid to the music. 'I remember watching the *Chart Show* one Saturday morning,' says Langan, 'and hearing "The Female of the Species" by Space. I became obsessed by the song; it seemed to say so much about our lives. We decided to have a contemporary soundtrack on *Cold Feet*, to use songs like snapshots that would create an emotional photo album of the characters' lives. I was very proprietorial about the music on the first couple of series, I'm sure I drove everyone mad. It was a very eclectic choice. We'd have Minnie Riperton, then Fatboy Slim. We cut from Andy Williams's verson of 'Can't Take My Eyes Off You' to the Fugees' version. I've still got all the *Cold Feet* CDs and I'm very proud of what we did with the music. It had real resonance.'

Langan stayed with *Cold Feet* for three series, seeing it through from six episodes to eight, then took an extended break before returning to England as a freelance producer. (She's subsequently produced *I Saw*

'I'm very proud of what we did with the music. It had real resonance.'

CHRISTINE LANGAN

You, starring Fay Ripley, and *Rescue Me* for the BBC.) She's now back at Granada developing new projects with Andy Harries.

Cold Feet has, among other things, provided a cryptic biography of its creator and those who worked closely with him. 'When we started out, the storylines were very directly inspired by our lives and our friends' lives,' says Christine Langan. 'As it went on, we had to cast the net a bit wide. At the beginning, for instance, Andy was very keen that we should get in a storyline about one of the couples trying to have children, because that was something that he was experiencing at the time. Mike and I weren't quite there yet, so it was a form of tourism for us – but as time went on all the major events in our lives were reflected in some way in *Cold Feet*.'

Now the show is definitely over. 'It was getting hard to find storylines,'

says Harries. 'Particularly for Helen and Jimmy – we didn't want to break them up, because otherwise none of the three couples would have stayed together. It's statistically true that at least one in three marriages survive divorce, so it was important to us to stay true to that. But once they were married with kids, there was nowhere else for them to go. There was endless pressure on us to increase the number of episodes per series, to go from eight to 15, but it wouldn't have been the same show. It would have turned into a soap. There's nothing wrong with soap, but *Cold Feet* was all about the details and the depth, and you can't do that if you're churning out 15 episodes. Something has to give. So rather than do that, we decided to put an end to it. We'd

'...after five series everyone's done everything with everyone else.'

ANDY HARRIES

gone through all the permutations that we could imagine without becoming unrealistic. You can only turn the Rubik's Cube so many times, and after five series everyone's done everything with everyone else. You can't stay truthful to a situation for that long.'

Adam's Other Women

Emma (Pooky Quesnel)

It's a sure sign of an impending mid-life crisis when a man in his 30s starts thinking he has a chance with a girl in her teens. Such things never worry Adam, though – and the moment he sets eyes on Emma, his fit, young, next-door neighbour, he starts to imagine the attraction is mutual. Emma, however, is only interested in going out jogging with Rachel; she's already got a boyfriend of her own age, and thinks of Adam as a cardigan-wearing father figure. The generation gap intervenes when Adam and Pete, on a desperate trawl through Manchester's clubs in search of their lost youth, find Emma and her boyfriend almost in the clutches of a drug dealer. Adam's a bit too ready with his fists – and it's only thanks to Emma (years his junior, but seemingly a good deal more mature) that he gets off scot free.

Callie (Natalie Roles)

Callie appears on the scene after Adam's placed an ad in the local paper's Meeting Place column. At first she seems like a sure bet: tall, blonde, beautiful, drives a Porsche. But their date swiftly degenerates into farce when Rachel and Danny turn up in the same restaurant. Callie, suspecting that Adam has set spies on her and storms out, leaving Adam single once more.

Rachel 2 (Rachel Fielding)

Things aren't going too well for Adam at the beginning of the second series; Rachel's left him, he's just got Amy off his hands, and then he hooks up with a new woman, a friend of Amy's whose name just happens to be... Rachel. There's an ugly moment when Rachel 1 finds Adam in bed with Rachel 2 (while Amy lounges around the bedroom in a nightie) – but the affair doesn't last, Rachel 2 settles in as Adam's sexless lodger and soon disappears with a barman she met at a club.

Amanda Wagstaff (Jo-Anne Knowles)

A face from Adam's past – his distant past, in fact. Amanda was his first girlfriend at school, and she's coming to a school reunion. Adam and Rachel, at this point, are theoretically 'just good friends', and Adam hopes that the old Williams magic will rekindle Amanda's fires. His hopes rise when he hears that her marriage is on the rocks, that she's left her husband – but are cruelly dashed when he discovers that she left him for another woman.

Jane Fitzpatrick
(Victoria Smurfit)

ADAM W 4 JANE F 20/6/83 TRUE LUV

Those few words carved on a bench above the Giants'
Causeway are all that's left of Adam's first great romance with
Jane, the girl he left behind in Northern Ireland. It was with
her that he lost his virginity, her that he was supposed to
come back to meet on New Year's Eve, 1999. He didn't come,
of course – but when he finds her again at his stag night, he
realises that this was more than just a teenage affair. And Jane's
still keen; keen enough to take him back to her flat for the
night, although he's too drunk to perform. That should have
been the end of that, but Jane rematerialises in Manchester
and seems to be stalking him. To Adam's horror, she befriends
Rachel and starts hanging round the house making leading
remarks. Adam still likes her, and toys with the idea of a
reunion – but he's a married man now, and he's desperate to
keep the truth from Rachel. Not that there's much to tell –
and, finally, Jane realises that she doesn't have a chance with
Adam, and returns to Ireland, no damage done.

Deborah (Helen Grace)

She drives a BMW, Adam drives an MG – and she doesn't
need to know that he's 'borrowed' it from his best friend Pete.
Nor does she need to know that Adam's not really
called Max Trendi. Nor that he's married. She might have
suspected something when he was unable to perform
sexually back at her flat, but 'Max' leaves before she can
ask any questions. That should be the end of that, but
Deborah turns up again at the Chester Race Course,
much to Adam's embarrassment.

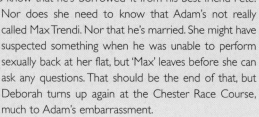

Jenny Gifford

(Fay Ripley)

Pete loves Jenny. Adam loves Jenny. Everyone else finds her, from time to time, a bit of a pain in the arse. She's great fun, always the first one to suggest a drink or a laugh, but she can also be a control-freak, and has an unfortunate tendency to whinge. She's a classic example of someone who got married too young, and who has never really been able to drag herself successfully into the adult world. That's okay for Pete: he'd be content with a simple life in which not too many demands are made on him. But that's not right for Jenny: she wants more than a cosy house in Manchester, a husband and a child. She doesn't know what she wants, though, and that's the trouble. Does she want a different man? Does she want Adam? Does she want a career? Does she want to travel? For Jenny, the grass is always greener on the other side of the fence. That makes her very hard to live with.

Jenny is a woman of strong, instinctive opinions. She has a very clear sense of self: she's a working-class woman, she's the salt of the earth, and as far as she's concerned she's honest and open and sensitive. While all this is true, it's balanced by the fact that she's often stubborn and prejudiced. When she feels uneasy or threatened by a situation, her natural response is to become aggressive and then to blame other people for winding her up. That's what happens at David's black-tie do, when she wrecks Natalie's dress. Of course, Jenny would never see that as being in any way her fault, and she won't apologise. As far as she's concerned, the rest of the world is always wrong, and Jenny Gifford is always right.

Her background hasn't done Jenny many favours. She lacked the opportunities available to her middle-class friends, and never had the educational background to make a mark in the professional world. So while Karen pursues a career in publishing, and Rachel gets ahead in advertising, Jenny is stuck in a series of menial, part-time jobs from which she takes great delight in getting sacked. She knows that she's too good for them, that secretarial work is beneath her - but instead of biding her time and working her way up through the ranks, she prefers to blow her top and walk out. She's so used to rejection

The life Jenny wanted...

...The life Jenny got.

in her professional life that she sets herself up for it; it's usually a case of resigning before she gets sacked. There's no doubt that Jenny's right: she's capable of great things, and whenever anyone has faith in her and gives her a chance she's incredibly capable, a born organiser. Her experience at Claibourne Hotels is a case in point: finally she meets someone who can see her true worth, and is willing to give her a chance. And that takes Jenny a long way - all the way to New York, and out of her marriage to Pete.

The same pattern applies to Jenny's personal life. When we first meet her, she's fast turning herself into a drudge, the kind of downtrodden Manchester housewife that's been in her family for generations. She's resentful, and she takes it out on Pete in a thousand ways. There's much more to Jenny than that, though, and her friends can see it; they all have happy memories of wild nights with Jenny, the ultimate good-time girl. But Jenny is terrified of being trapped, of failing to realise her potential, and that leads only to frustration and bitterness.

Her first attempt to find real fulfilment is in motherhood. She's absolutely determined to have a baby, because she feels that this is a role that will give her some value in the eyes of society, and at which she can excel. She bullies Pete into

MIKE BULLEN ON *Jenny*

If you knew Jenny in real life, you'd love her madly and she'd drive you mad. She winds people up all the time. She's the kind of woman who speaks without engaging her brain — she just says whatever comes into her head. She thinks that's being honest, but there is such a thing as being too honest. She's very attractive for that reason, because she says what she thinks and isn't inhibited like the rest of the characters: she's certainly a fully paid-up human being. She'll never play second fiddle to anyone. But Jenny's problem is that she got married too young. She's a bright woman who didn't get on with education, and she realises later in life that she's got potential. That's what disrupts her marriage.

fatherhood - but then he always has to be pushed into anything. And then, when the baby's on the way, Jenny gets terrible cold feet. She's terrified of motherhood, she's not sure if she's ready to make the necessary sacrifices. And when Adam Junior finally comes along, he's not enough to satisfy her. Soon she's frustrated again, desperately looking for ways out.

'I'm meant to be subtle about this, but sod that. What's his name, what does he earn, how big's his willy?'
JENNY GIFFORD

Discovering that Pete is having an affair is all Jenny needs to break up the happy home. She's certainly the injured party, but there's never any suggestion that she might forgive Pete for the sake of their son. She wants to move on, and getting rid of Pete is a necessary stepping stone. She only comes back home when she's desperate - but let's hope that this time she'll be willing on occasion to entertain the idea that she isn't always right about everything.

Jenny is an impetuous character in many ways, and that's what makes her attractive. She can be obstreperous and downright rude, but she can also bring a ray of sunshine into any situation. She's refreshingly direct in a world where most of her peers are dishonest and defensive. Jenny will always call a spade a spade, even when that is the very worst thing to do. She believes in plain speaking at whatever cost. If she finds out something about one of her friends, she makes it her business to let the world know, even if by doing so she's destroying other people's happiness. Jenny's a bull in a china shop, and sometimes you have to admire her for it. But not always.

Of all the *Cold Feet* characters, Jenny is the most unhappy for the longest time. But that's because she's an early developer. She got married young, she became a mother first, and she was the first to become dissatisfied with her life. Her marriage to Pete was going wrong in the early days, and they've made each other's lives hell over five series. Jenny knows in her heart that Pete's the man for her, that they should be married, not just for the sake of their son - but she finds it hard to accept that this is really all life has to offer.

Loves
♡ Having fun
♡ Plain speaking
♡ Fantasising
♡ Adventure

Hates
☾ Others' superiority
☾ Boring jobs
☾ Keeping secrets
☾ Pete's lack of ambition

Homecoming... Jenny returns to Manchester.

Fay Ripley

(Jenny Gifford)

The *Cold Feet* producers spent a long time looking for an actress to play Jenny before they found Fay Ripley. 'Well, they made the mistake of looking for a real northerner,' says Fay. 'They should have started in Surrey. What they needed was a nice Weybridge girl. It's obvious, isn't it?'

Fay already knew the casting director, Kate Rhodes James, from drama school, and knew both James Nesbitt and John Thomson socially. 'I assumed, of course, that I was up for the role of Rachel. I'd read the script and I just thought naturally they wanted me for the part of the pretty, sexy one – not the northern bird married to John Thomson. That wouldn't be right at all!' When she discovered that she was actually reading for the role of Jenny, Fay assumed that she wouldn't get the job. 'I was very relaxed at that audition, because I'd decided I didn't stand much of a chance. I just went in and mucked about with John a bit, and that was that. I'd absolutely recommend that to anyone going for a job interview: if you think you've got nothing to lose, you'll be more likely to get it.'

There was one stumbling block, though: the accent. 'For the audition I managed to bodge together a sort of Manchester accent, but once we started filming I really had to work on it. Of course I suggested that maybe Jenny should be from Surrey after all, but that was not up for discussion: she and Pete had to be the Mancunian characters in the show. So I then spent as much time as possible pretending to be interested in the locals. I'd talk for hours to people, disguising my lack of interest in what they were saying, just so I could study the voice. 'Oh really, how fascinating, do tell me more...' In the end it really convinced people. The accent was good enough for me to get a job as the voice of Manchester car parks one Christmas, so obviously the mayor was fooled. You'd hear Jenny's voice going "Please remember to take your ticket with you..." booming over the tannoys.'

During the long pause between the pilot and the first series, Ripley had become obsessed by the idea of keeping the role. 'Everyone involved in the pilot realised that the show was good enough for several series, and we became desperate to get a commission. It was a very fraught time, and I think that if we'd known then just how much *Cold Feet* was going to do for our careers, it would have been even worse. When that first series came along, it was tremendous, and I still think it's the best series of *Cold Feet*. It was perfectly balanced. It focused on all three couples, whereas the pilot had really been about Adam and Rachel with the rest of us in the background, John and me as the tubby ones in the nasty floral shirts. In the series, we had much more to get our teeth into.'

For Ripley, that involved undergoing pregnancy and childbirth. 'I was very proud of the scenes in which Jenny expressed her anxiety about becoming a mother, because in most TV comedy and drama you only ever see motherhood as something wonderful and beautiful. I thought it was good when we made it, and now that I'm a mother myself (Ripley gave birth to a daughter, Parker, at the end of 2002) I can honestly say that it was spot-on. That scene in which Jenny pushes Pete up against the mirror and tells him how frightened she is will always be my favourite scene in *Cold Feet*. We were really up against the schedules at the time, and that scene was just tagged on the end to fill up some time, but it came out so well. It summed Jenny up for me: a woman who says things that people don't always want to hear. She can sometimes be funny, sometimes irritating, sometimes really unlikeable, but that always gave her an edge.'

The second series saw the disintegration of Pete and Jenny's marriage; in the third series she was having affairs and trying to move on. 'By the time we got into the subsequent series, the couples were taking it in turns to be miserable. When it was our turn, I was quite pleased; it gives you a wider variety of material. The way Mike Bullen wrote that relationship was very realistic; they split up, they got back together, but there was never a happy ending for Pete and Jenny. However hard they tried to make it work, the underlying problems were always there. At the very end of the final series, there's some hope that they'll make it – which is just as well, otherwise it would just be too bleak.'

After a couple of rounds of separation and reunion, Ripley felt that she'd gone as far as she could with the character of Jenny, and decided to leave *Cold Feet* after the third series. 'I just couldn't work with John Thomson any more! Actually, there were a lot of reasons for leaving, and they all sound like cliches. It seemed like a big risk at the time, but I had other jobs I wanted to do, and I would have had to turn them down if I'd stayed with *Cold Feet*. And I just felt enough was enough with Jenny. I didn't want people to start thinking "Oh God, here she comes again, the stroppy northern one". So I left. I never regretted it. It was the right thing to do.'

Ripley wanted Jenny to go with a bang, and begged Mike Bullen to kill the character off. 'He refused to do that, so then we started negotiating. I said 'Okay, how about if she loses both of her legs?' No, he wasn't having that. 'Her arms? One arm?' No: in the end he decided that she'd leave because she was really good at her job and wanted to move to New York. So that was a pretty big climb-down for me, as you can imagine, but I'm glad now because it meant that I could come back for the last two episodes. And I was glad of the work by then, because I was so heavily pregnant that nobody else would employ me. You can

see just by the size of my bottom, let alone my stomach, that I was very, very pregnant.

'Going back to *Cold Feet* was quite strange, because I felt that I'd never been away. I'd done one episode of the fourth series in 2001, then I went off and did *I Saw You* with the same production team, then *Stretford Wives*, then *Dead Gorgeous*, and I was always seeing the other *Cold Feet* actors for promotional things. And then in 2002 I was back in Manchester being Jenny again, staying at the same hotel, making the same train journey with the same delays. It was kind of nostalgic, and I'm very glad that I came back in so that the team was together again, but a show like *Cold Feet* doesn't just end when you shoot the last episode. It will go on and on, and it will always be a part of our lives, whatever we do.'

Series 2

26 Sept - 31 Oct 1999 ⑤ 6 episodes

And this is where things start to go **really wrong**. Rachel's back in town, but without a baby - and it's a long time before Adam can understand what she's been through, let alone forgive her. For much of the second series, Adam and Rachel's relationship is on the rocks, and it's not until Adam's major health scare with **testicular cancer** that the two of them realise that life's too short to let mistakes get in the way of true love.

But before Adam and Rachel can get back together again, there's the small matter of Jenny and Pete to deal with. Jenny has realised that she **doesn't** love Pete any more, and increasingly she finds that her feelings are turning towards Adam. And when Adam's single, that's a very dangerous situation for Jenny to be in. Nothing happens — but while Pete's given the cold shoulder, he finds comfort in the arms of his colleague (and Adam's ex-girlfriend) Amy. This turns into a full-blown **affair**, and when Jenny finds out it marks the end of the Gifford marriage.

And the cracks are beginning to show in the Marsden marriage as well. Karen's had itchy feet for a long time, but has always put her family first. Now, however, she's feeling the strain. She starts smoking joints, getting **tattoos**… but that's small fry compared to what's coming up in later series. For now, there are more important things to consider — like organising a group holiday to Lindisfarne to see in the new millennium, and to wonder what the future has in store.

Series 2

Episode 1

Rachel's back in town – but where's the baby? ... David's lost his job, but isn't cut out to be a househusband ... Jenny can't ignore her growing feelings for Adam

Several months have passed without a word from Rachel. Adam's written to her every day (but hasn't posted the letters); she's not even been in touch with Karen, her oldest friend. She's due to give birth any day now, and the friends are wondering what kind of baby she'll have – and, more importantly, who the father is. It should be clear enough: if the baby's white, it's Adam's. If it's black, it's Kris's. Case closed.

Adam and Amy, Pete and Jenny, two matches that definitely weren't made in heaven!

Adam's finding it very hard to move on. He can't stop thinking about Rachel, and about the life they could have had together as parents. He fantasises about a daughter: maybe they'd call her Amy. Even when Pete and Jenny set him up on a blind date, he can't stop going on about Rachel and the baby. Astonishingly, his date – a workmate of Pete's who just happens to be called Amy – finds this kind of behaviour attractive, and takes Adam up on his offer of a drink after dinner. And so, on a park bench with a bottle of Scotch, Adam and Amy find comfort in each other's arms... And then again another five times during the night.

Bad news *chez* Marsden: David's been made redundant, and is finding it very hard to adjust to the loss of status. On top of the humiliation of having to do the 'Dead Man's Walk' through his office, he's terrified of what the neighbours will think – and has already decided that he's going to put on a suit and leave the house every day, just so nobody suspects he's lost his job.

Into this volatile situation walks Rachel, with her usual tact and timing, unexpected, unannounced and, seemingly, unaccompanied by a baby. She's come back to tie up a few loose ends, the biggest of those being Adam – and so Karen volunteers to find out exactly what Adam's up to. An unexpected visit to the house finds Adam unshaven, bleary-eyed and smelling of whisky, with the sexually voracious Amy calling him back to bed: not exactly the picture of a man who wants his ex-girlfriend back. Rachel assumes that he's got over her, and that for her, too, it's time to move on.

And then, one afternoon, Pete spots Rachel pushing a baby round a supermarket. True to form, Pete jumps to conclusions: obviously the baby must be Rachel's, despite the fact that it has unmistakeably oriental features. Black or white would have made sense, but Japanese? The baby, of course, belongs to a friend of Karen's, and Rachel's just looking after it – but Pete, fancying himself as a superspy, grabs a disposable camera and is soon presenting the evidence to Adam. Fired by wishful thinking, Adam deduces that the baby clearly isn't black, therefore isn't Kris's – and therefore must be his. Yes, after all that heartbreak and uncertainty, he is the father of Rachel's child, and he will do everything in his power to get her back.

First things first: he has to get rid of Amy. But Amy's not so easily budged. She sows doubt in Adam's mind: why hasn't Rachel been in touch with him, if it's his child? Does she really want him back? Isn't it likely that she, like him, has already found somebody else? This time it's Jenny who sets off on a fact-finding mission – and what she has to report is music to Adam's ears. No, there's no

'What Jennifer wants, Jennifer gets. I'm easy, she's happy.'

Pete's recipe for a happy marriage

new bloke, and yes, she would like to see Adam again. Torn between satisfaction and regret – ever since that kiss, she has quite fancied Adam for herself – Jenny passes the news on to a delighted Adam. The stage is set, it seems, for the big reunion.

David's finding it harder than he expected to be a househusband. Josh is a demanding little lad, and David's a hopeless, impatient father. He can't be bothered to play with the child, doesn't want to look at his drawings, doesn't even know where his nursery is. He's completely preoccupied with his own work situation. Time and hope are running out; every call he makes meets with a polite rebuff, and David is becoming desperate.

And then, out of the blue, Natalie calls – awful Natalie who's caused David so much trouble in the past, and who gave him his marching orders from his job. She's quit the company, she tells him, and been headhunted for a great new job – and she wants to take David with her as her number two. Good money, good pension, share options, the lot. David is delighted, and so absorbed in his own good fortune that he doesn't see baby Josh toddling off towards the road... David snatches him from the path of a speeding car just in time to save his life, and begins to realise that, perhaps, there's more to life than work.

Adam has gone into overdrive in preparation for his reunion with Rachel. He's even gone so far as to redecorate the spare room as a nursery, complete with Pete and Jenny's spare cot and Peter Rabbit mobile. Rachel turns up for dinner, and the mood seems perfect for a happy ending. But first he has something to show her: the baby's room. Rachel bursts into tears, and tells Adam that there is no baby; when she got to London, she had an abortion. Adam is horrified; 'I loved that baby!' he shouts. The evening is over.

Jenny trudges home to Pete; he, too, has been redecorating, and proudly shows off the living room. Jenny's unimpressed. 'Tell me honestly,' says Pete, suspecting nothing, 'what do you think?' 'I think I don't love you any more,' replies Jenny.

> ## Real Life
>
> 👁 The scene in which Josh is nearly run over was inspired by an accident that befell one of Andy Harries's sons. 'It provoked a huge rethink about the priorities in my life. Of all the characters, David is the one I most identify with.'

Poor old David is not cut out to be a househusband.

Episode 2

Pete comes to terms with the collapse of his marriage ... Jenny confesses to Adam that she's in love with him ... David discovers the joys of fatherhood ... Rachel's dreams of a happy reunion go badly wrong

Can it be true? Does Jenny really not love Pete any more? She sounded like she meant it at the time – but, as she points out to Pete, she'd had a lot to drink, it was her time of the month, she was in a bad mood. But Pete doesn't believe a word of it. He knows in his heart that something is wrong. He just has to find out what.

Things aren't any better for Adam, who's in a bad way after discovering that Rachel got rid of the baby that might have been his. He pours out his heart to Pete, who, as usual, is the stoic, supportive best mate – and doesn't let on that he's got troubles of his own. It's up to Jenny to tell Adam what's going on, and then Adam, in a stroke of inspiration that's stupid even by his standards, leaves the cordless phone on the kitchen table so that Pete can listen in to Jenny's

In her dreams! Jenny and Adam glide through Venice on a Gondola.

Pete attacks Adam... again

explanation. Yes, she says, there is someone else. It's someone that Pete knows. Someone arrogant, funny, good looking... Just in time, Adam realises that Jenny's about to name him. He can't afford for Pete to overhear, so does the one thing he can think of to silence Jenny – he snogs her. Pete's not to be put off the scent so easily and turns detective; he finds Jenny's diary, reads her confession of love for Adam, and goes storming round to Adam's office to confront him in front of all his colleagues. A swift right hook sends Adam sprawling to the floor, and Pete storms out threatening much worse if Adam goes anywhere near Jenny ever again.

While Karen's going out to work every day, David's staying at home and discovering the joys of fatherhood. The near-accident at the end of the last episode has shaken him badly, and he realises that his own self-absorption nearly cost him his son. But typically, David's over-reacted. He's taking Josh out to Blackpool beach, treating him to days in the park, disrupting his routine and making Ramona one very unhappy Spanish nanny. Well, says David, there's a simple solution to that: let's just get rid of Ramona, and save ourselves a lot of money. Karen begins to smell a rat.

BT or not BT

ⓖ The scene in which Pete confronts Adam in his office was filmed at the BT offices in Manchester – and the extras were real BT employees.

ⓖ It's John Thomson's favourite scene from the series, 'because a lot of people believed that I smacked Jimmy for real. It looks a lot closer than it really was.'

David's idea of a good day out
with his son.

Things are not going well for Adam. He's lost Rachel, he's lost his best mate, and he's still got insatiable Amy making impossible demands on him night after night. Things have got to be sorted out. He turns up at Pete and Jenny's to take the bull by the horns. 'Look, Jen,' he says, 'I like you. I love you, like a sister. But Jen, for Christ's sakes, you're my best mate's wife.' Jenny slaps him round the face and storms out of the room, leaving Adam to conclude a fragile truce with Pete. They stalk off to the pub, just like old times... almost.

It seems as if things are back on track. Adam's got his eye on a new girlfriend, a friend of Amy's who needs a place to stay and agrees to be his lodger (it doesn't help that her name is Rachel...). He gives Amy her marching orders, but forgets to take back his spare set of keys. Meanwhile, Rachel is telling Karen that she's made a mistake, and that she wants to get back together with Adam. If only she can think of the right words to say.

Karen calls David's bluff over a dinner party to which she's invited Natalie and her husband, George. It soon emerges that Karen knows that Natalie offered David a job, and that David, chastened by his experiences with Josh, turned it down. Karen explains to David that he can still be a good father even if he's holding down a full-time job; it's just a question of finding a balance. David sees sense for once, and accepts Natalie's offer.

Rachel arrives at Adam's, with her big speech all prepared, rehearsing in her mind the wonderful reunion scene that will surely follow. But, as usual, things don't quite go according to plan. Adam's upstairs in the spare room getting down to business with his new lodger, Rachel 2. Amy meanwhile, is also in Adam's house; she let herself in with the spare keys and is now in his bed, dressed in some revealing lingerie, awaiting his return home. A beautiful romantic evening descends rapidly into cruel farce. Rachel arrives to find Adam, naked, with not one but two scantily-clad women. Not waiting for an explanation, Rachel flees.

Grand Canal

Jenny's fantasy of her and Adam in a Venetian gondola was, inevitably, filmed on the Manchester Ship Canal on a freezing cold day. James Nesbitt was naked apart from a strategically-placed cushion.

Episode 3

Rachel's got a toyboy ... Karen and David's anniversary
doesn't go quite according to plan ... Pete goes Outward
Bound with Amy ... Adam's looking for love in the small ads

Pete and Amy's romantic weekend!

Rachel's decided that she can't spend the rest of her life regretting her past actions, and so she gets her old job back and tries to make a new start in life. She's certainly not short of opportunities: she hasn't been back in the job for five minutes before the men in the office are buzzing around her like bees round honey. Two of her younger colleagues, Patrick and Danny, make a bet that they can get her into bed by the end of the week.

Adam's finding it harder to put Rachel behind him. He's still going over and over the events of that disastrous night when Rachel turned up on his doorstep only to find him on the brink of what appeared to be an orgy. And to make matters worse, Rachel 2 has decided that it would be better off to keep their relationship strictly landlord and tenant, and to push the point home she's taken up with a very fit barman. The only way to even the score, Adam decides, is to find a proper girlfriend of his own. Shouldn't be difficult... should it? But somehow the old Williams magic doesn't seem to be working the way it used to, and finally Adam takes Jenny's advice and takes a look at the Meeting Place column in the local paper. This should be a piece of cake, thinks Adam – but somehow he can't seem to find anyone that appeals. There's only one thing for it: he'll have to place a personal ad of his own.

David is feeling very pleased with himself: not only is he back at work, but he's also managed to remember his wedding anniversary, and is planning a surprise treat for Karen: a weekend in London, posh hotel, nice restaurant, West End show, the works. There's only one fly in the ointment: unknown to David, Karen is also planning an anniversary treat, a weekend in Paris for two, and his enlisted his boss Natalie's help in setting it up. David will be sent to Paris to visit a client – but will be met on the plane by his wife.

Life at Pete and Jenny's goes from bad to worse. Adam's no longer coming between them, but still things haven't improved. They spend night after night staring at the TV with nothing to say to each other, each brooding over their private resentments. Pete badly needs a friend – and, as luck would have it, he finds one. Amy, Adam's recent ex, is in a bad way too, bursting into tears over the photocopier; despite the fact that she claims to have got over Adam, she still has his picture as her screensaver. A comforting hug in the stationery cupboard is witnessed by a nosy secretary, and soon the rumours begin to fly around the office. Amy doesn't seem to think this is a problem, and jumps at the chance to spend some time with Pete on an Outward Bound course that the firm's organised to spot potential managers. Pete's not keen – but anything's got to be better than sitting at home all weekend with a resentful wife.

Against her better judgement, Rachel has started dating Danny, one of the lads at work, seven years her junior. At first it's just a bit of fun, but when she discovers that he actually knows a bit about Japanese cinema and can talk with some confidence about Akira Kurosawa, she's hooked. Things are going well until she discovers that he's only been taking her out on dates in order to win a £20 bet with Patrick. Furious, she dumps him: only to discover that the deadline for the bet has passed, that Danny really likes her and is determined to make up for his mistakes. And so, the next morning, a sheepish Danny comes down to breakfast with David and Karen, to face the inevitable jokes about his age ('There are Coco Pops in the cupboard').

Adam's received a pile of responses to his ad, which he's sorted into three piles: yes, no and maybe. With Jenny's encouragement, he picks one from the 'yes' pile and gives her a call; to his astonishment the woman, Callie, sounds quite nice and agrees to go for dinner

G.S.O.H

In the original script, David and Karen's anniversary plans went wrong and they never met up. At the last minute it was decided to bring them together in Paris – so the actors and a minimal crew caught the Eurostar and filmed a brief scene with Notre Dame in the background. The floodlights on the cathedral were switched off before they'd finished – so the crew improvised with their car headlights.

Speed-dating. Adam's date with
Callie lasts all of thirty minutes.

with him. Adam awaits her in a smart Japanese restaurant – only to find that Rachel and Danny are dining at the adjacent table. The bickering begins instantly as the two men begin to fight over Rachel; but then Callie turns up. Tall, blonde, beautiful, holding the keys to a Porsche. First round to Adam.

Things go quickly wrong, however, when Callie realises that the people at the next table are friends of Adam's. Has he placed them there to spy on her? She walks out in a huff, seemingly unconcerned by the fact that she had placed her own spies at a nearby table as well. To make the evening perfect, Adam and Rachel have another of their great restaurant rows, she slaps his face and leaves.

Karen and David's travel plans nearly go awry. Karen ends up on a train to London; David ends up alone in Paris, wondering what happened to the business trip that Natalie had supposedly sent him on. And then, just as he's about to give up, his wife appears at his side. For once, two people are entirely happy together, and they have a wonderful weekend.

Far, far away, in a Travelodge somewhere in the north-west of England, Pete and Amy are making the first tentative steps in an affair. Both of them are thinking about someone else; Amy is still marking time over Adam, and Pete phones Jenny from the hotel room to tell her that he loves her.

'Do you really want Josh to grow up thinking his Mummy's a Hell's Angel?'

DAVID MARSDEN

Episode 4

Secrets and revelations at the school reunion ... Karen gets a tattoo ... Pete confesses that he's having an affair with Amy ... Rachel and Adam are friends again, and both single

Adam, Pete and Jenny receive invitations to a school reunion; it's 15 years since they left, and the Class of 84 is gathering once again. Pete and Jenny are keen: it was in the school hall that they had their first proper kiss, and it seems like a good time to rekindle the flame (despite the fact that, unknown to Jenny, Pete is now having an affair with Amy). Adam's not so sure: he's got nothing to show for his life since leaving school. 'I'm not even divorced!', he moans to Pete. And, worse still, he doesn't have a date. Looking on the bright side, however, he realises that Amanda Wagstaff might be there – Amanda, his first girlfriend, who should, by rights, have grown up into a very attractive woman. Pete fans the flames by telling Adam that Amanda's marriage has broken up, and in theory she's footloose and fancy free. All Adam has to do now is find a date.

Karen has an out-of-body experience during a life-threateningly dull dinner party with her boring, bourgeois friends. She suddenly realises that they're stupid, materialistic and shallow – and, worse still, she fits right in. An emergency call to Rachel (who's still staying with Karen and David) procures a small amount of dope which Rachel had hidden in her bedside table. To the astonishment of her guests (and to David's utter horror), Karen skins up at the dinner table and proceeds to get happily stoned.

This proves to be a life-changing experience for Karen. Within days she's cleaning out her closet, chucking all her designer dresses into black bin-bags to go to the Oxfam shop, passing on some of the better pieces to Ramona, and generally trying to break out of the middle-class trap she's fallen into. In a moment of madness, Karen and Rachel drag each other to a tattoo parlour, whence Karen emerges with a gecko etched into the small of her back, and Rachel emerges in excruciating pain.

David, of course, does not approve of his 'new' wife. Her beautiful expensive dresses will end up on the backs of Africans; 'They're already as thin as supermodels. Now they can dress like them.' She's smoking dope, she's got a tattoo; does she really want Josh to grow up thinking his Mummy's a Hell's Angel? Karen rather acerbically reminds David that, due to a misunderstanding with a

Ouch! Karen changes her image.

hand-me-down Prada dress, he's already groped Ramona's bum, so he's hardly a model citizen himself.

Pete's affair with Amy is going a little bit further than he'd planned. After their night of passion in a motel, they're now seeing each other in the evenings, forcing Pete to creep home with limp excuses about the audit taking a little longer than he'd imagined. Jenny suspects nothing; she could never imagine that Pete would have an affair.

The deception is too much for Pete, though, and he decides to confide in Adam – never a wise move. Adam's outraged, and threatens to tell Jenny. Pete makes him promise to keep it secret, and Adam gives his word. Even Pete realises that's not worth much...

The night of the reunion rolls around, and the gang gathers in the old school hall. Rachel's stood Adam up; she's in such pain with her tattoo that she's had to go to see a doctor, and sends Karen along as her substitute. Adam's not displeased; at least he has a beautiful woman on his arm when he bumps into Amanda Wagstaff. But his hopes in that direction are dashed when Amanda points out her new partner – and it's a woman. Maybe that explains why they never got beyond first base.

Stung by disappointment, Adam retreats into the gents with Karen, who rolls a joint and shows off her new tattoo. The mood seems to invite confidences, and so Adam blurts out the 'secret' about Pete and Amy. Karen is horrified; they must tell Jenny, she says. But Jenny and Pete are having such a good time, dancing like fools to the 80s disco and generally reliving their youth. Is honesty really the best policy?

Rachel turns up late, and tells Adam that she's single again; her relationship with 21-year-old Danny is over. Adam's delighted; for him, the spark is still there, and he hopes that they might get back together again. He introduces her to his old English teacher Malcolm Chacksfield, an attractive man in his mid–40s, and is then horrified when Rachel gets off with him. 'Your last boyfriend was pre-pubescent; this one's practically due his bus pass!' he moans. 'Are you trying to do all the seven ages of man?' Rachel reminds him that he has no right to criticise her choice of partners; after all, they're not going out any more, are they?

Karen takes Jenny to one side and tells her that her husband is having an affair. But before Jenny can confront Pete, Adam intervenes and gives it to her straight. Why does she think Pete is seeing Amy? After all, it was Jenny who said she didn't love him, Jenny who fell in love with Adam... All that Pete's doing is finding a little comfort outside an unhappy relationship. Jenny sees his point, and doesn't tell Pete that she knows what he's up to. Adam, for his part, promises to get Pete back on track.

Adam and Rachel are officially friends again. Her date with Mr Chacksfield comes to nothing; she's horrified to discover that he dresses like a teacher even out of school hours, and does a runner from the bar where they were meant to meet. A friendly trip to the cinema very nearly develops into something more, but Adam and Rachel part at the doorstep, both wishing they had made a move.

Pete, despite his promises to finish with Amy, is still 'working late'. Jenny's suspicions are aroused when she calls him at the office and finds he's already left. Furious, she takes the baby and marches round to Amy's flat – just in time to catch Pete coming out. She dumps baby Adam in Amy's arms and marches off down the street, the sound of her own child's crying ringing in her ears.

Mr Chacksfield's dress sense (or rather lack of it!) proved too
much for Rachel and their relationship was short-lived.

SCENE 8 INT
SET DAVID & KAREN'S DINING ROOM

THE DINNER PARTY HAS REACHED COFFEE STAGE. EACH OF THE
PARTICIPANTS ALSO HAS A LIQUEUR. DAVID AND MARK PUFF CIGARS.
AS BEFORE, CONVERSATION IS LIVELY.

NATASHA: I love auctions! And there's always the chance
you'll find a bargain. Last week I stumbled on a painting
and I think it might be by the Norwich School.

JAMES: (TEASING HER) Well,it's of a Norwich School.

THE MEN CHORTLE. NATASHA TURNS TO KAREN FOR SUPPORT.

NATASHA: Karen, you studied art history...

ALL EYES TURN TO KAREN AND ARE RATHER ASTONISHED TO FIND HER
IN THE LATTER STAGES OF MAKING A HUGE JOINT. SHE'S JUST
ATTEMPTING TO LIGHT IT, PUFFING IN AS SHE HOLDS A MATCH TO
THE END. JUST AS SHE TAKES HER FIRST DEEP TOKE, SHE CATCHES
THEM ALL STARING AT HER. SHE PRESUMES THEY'RE WAITING TO BE
OFFERED SOME.

KAREN: (HOLDING JOINT OUT) Oh I'm awfully sorry. Would
anybody like some?

DAVID IS SPEECHLESS. JAMES, NATASHA AND LAURA MAKE
APOLOGETIC NOISES. MARK SAYS NOTHING.

JAMES/NATASHA/LAURA: (SIMULTANEOUSLY): I don't thanks.
(JAMES) Now that we've got kids (NATASHA) I've got to be up
early... (LAURA)

KAREN SHRUGS - SUIT YOURSELVES AND PUFFS CONTENTEDLY ON HER
SPLIFF. THE OTHERS JUST WATCH.

CUT TO
SCENE 9 INT
SET DAVID & KAREN'S BATHROOM

DAVID AND KAREN ARE GETTING READY FOR BED. DAVID IS
EXTREMELY WORKED UP, AGITATEDLY STRIDING AS KAREN BRUSHES
HER TEETH.

DAVID: Were you out of your mind?!!

KAREN: Briefly. I don't think it was particularly good stuff.

DAVID: I have never been so embarrassed!

KAREN: Oh, come on, David! ('HAVE YOU FORGOTTEN?') School nativity play? One of the three wise men wet themselves. (DAVID'S ASTONISHED STARE - 'HOW DO YOU KNOW ABOUT THAT?!') Your mother told me.

DAVID: You do not offer marijuana at dinner parties!

KAREN: You offered Cuban cigars. Which smell a damn sight worse.

DAVID: Yes, but they're not illegal.

KAREN: In America they are. (OFF DAVID'S NON-FORGIVING LOOK) I'm sorry David, but I was bored. Bored bloody rigid.

DAVID: Well you were certainly quiet. Perhaps if you'd got a bit more involved...

KAREN: (UNAPOLIGETICALLY) I'm sorry. I had no interest in discussing nannies. Again.

DAVID: That wasn't all we talked about.

KAREN: Or skiing hilidays, house prices or private education.

DAVID: Well, you could have started a conversation of your own.

KAREN: David, I tried.

DAVID: (REMEMBERING, FLATLY) Oh, yes.

SCENE 10 INT
SET DAVID & KAREN'S DINING ROOM

EARLIER IN THE EVENING. KAREN IS DISHING OUT THE DESSERTS WHICH ARE THEN BEING PASSED ALONG THE TABLE.

KAREN: Did you know that there's a tribe in Borneo, right, where instead of shaking hands on a deal, men masturbate one another?

SILENCE. NOBODY QUITE KNOWS HOW TO REACT TO THIS TITBIT OF INFORMATION. NATASHA IS SO STUNNED SHE DOESN'T NOTICE THAT THE CREAM SHE IS POURING ONTO HER DESSERT IS ABOUT TO OVERFLOW.

Episode 5

Jenny throws Pete out of the house ... David's charming younger brother turns up out of the blue ... Adam discovers that he's got testicular cancer ... Rachel makes a big decision

Out with the old... but before long Pete is forced back into the marital home.

Jenny's taking a hard line on Pete's infidelity: she's chucking him out of the house, and won't even let him take a suitcase with him. Pete puts a few clothes into plastic bin bags and goes to stay in Adam's spare room. But Pete's determined to put the past behind him and start again with Jenny, so as a gesture of goodwill he quits his job so that he will never have to see Amy again. Jenny doesn't take kindly to this: who will pay the mortgage now? Is she doomed to the life of an impoverished single mother? The future looks bleak for both of them.

An unexpected (and very attractive) visitor turns up at Karen and David's house: it's David's younger brother, Nick, the black sheep of the family, who starts flirting with Rachel the moment he meets her. David is less than pleased that Nick's turned up; he'll only be wanting money, he says, and indeed within a very short space of time Nick's asked for £5000 to pay back a loan from his parents. The internet company he started up has folded, and he doesn't know where else to go. David, who's always resented his parents' coddling of his younger brother, has no intention of parting with the money, but says he'll think about it.

Adam learns all about this during a particularly aggressive squash game with David, during which he gets a ball in the balls and ends the match doubled up in agony on the floor. The pain persists, and when Adam manages to pick up a young lady at a local bar, she's horrified to discover that his testicles are black and swollen. 'They shouldn't be that colour,' she says, 'Well, not unless the rest of you is.' She advises Adam to get himself checked out, before she hastens out of the house.

So Adam goes for a check-up, and the doctor gives him bad news: she's concerned by a swelling that may pre-date the accident, and advises him to go for a scan. The results are shocking: Adam has testicular cancer, and there's a good chance that the tumour is malignant. Devastated by the news, Adam breaks down in the back of a cab and confesses his fears to the driver, who turns out to be a sympathetic listener and won't even charge him for the ride.

Rachel, predictably, is rather taken with the roguish Nick. He's the exact opposite of David: he votes labour, he's always voted labour, he likes Massive Attack and Irvine Welsh and experimental theatre... all of which leads to a kiss under a lamp post, so intense that Rachel doesn't even notice the dog turds strewn over the pavement. It takes Jenny to point them out — but then she's seeing the bad side of life all around her at the moment. She's decided to get a divorce; it's not just that Pete's had an affair, it's because she realises that they no longer belong together.

Putting thoughts into action, Jenny forces Pete to move all his stuff out of the

house and tells him that any objections he may have will be settled by the lawyers. Pete and Jenny are rowing like children, much to the distress of Adam, who can't bear the idea of his two best friends splitting up so acrimoniously. And so, in order to bring them to their senses, he announces that he's got cancer. At first they think it's a joke – but Adam is deadly serious.

Adam's rushed into surgery, and as the anaesthetic kicks in he has a vision of Rachel, and realises that she is the love of his life. When he comes to, he sees her sitting by his bed, and imagines at first that he's still hallucinating... But no, it's really her. She's there because she cares about him. Whatever they once had is still there... And then the rest of the gang arrives, desperate to comfort Adam but managing to make a fist of it (perhaps Pete shouldn't have mentioned that Adolf Hitler only had one ball). Rachel moves back in to Adam's flat in order to nurse him, and says that, after all, perhaps they should get back together. But is it just because of Adam's illness? 'I think we missed our moment,' says Adam, regretfully.

David is playing cat and mouse with his brother, leading him to believe that the loan will be forthcoming only to tell him, finally, that he needs to stand on his own two feet. Karen thinks otherwise. She persuades David that he's

Balls

The testicular cancer storyline was partly inspired by the writings of John Diamond, who documented his illness with unflinching honesty.

The nightmare scene, in which Adam is being chased down a Manchester street by a giant bouncing testicle, was inspired by the opening sequence of The Prisoner, in which a giant ball bounces across Port Meirion beach.

withholding the money for selfish reasons, that the only people who will suffer will be David's parents, and that it would be better to be generous while he can. David, realising that she is right, writes a cheque, and Nick clears off – but not before suggesting to Rachel that maybe they should try going out together.

This gives Rachel food for thought. Does she really want to start all over again with someone new? Or does she want to get back together with the man who, despite everything, still loves her? Her mind made up, she barges into Adam's bathroom and announces that she loves him and will do anything for him. He tells her to get into the bath. She does, fully clothed.

Pete and Jenny, chastened by Adam's near-death experience, decide to patch things up. Amy's explained things to Jenny, and has moved to Bristol: the affair's over. Pete gets his job back and assumes that the rest will follow – but Jenny's not so sure.

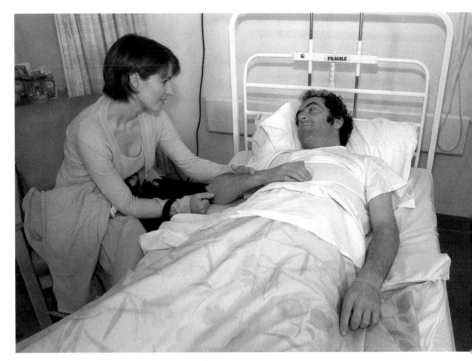

Life's too short... Adam and Rachel sort out their differences.

Episode 6

David's rented a castle for the New Year... Adam and Pete have a near death experience... Karen has some news... Will Pete and Jenny ever resolve their differences?

The new century is approaching, and the gang is headed for Lindisfarne for a party in a castle organised by David. It's a wonderful place, cut off from the mainland and high tide, magical and romantic... and, for David, full of bittersweet memories of childhood holidays. But this is where he wants to spend the New Year, with the people he really considers to be his friends (plus Ramona, of course). The others are thrilled; none of them had any particular plans for the big day, and are more than happy to be treated to a long weekend in this extraordinary location. There's just one condition: nobody is allowed to mention the 'M' word. No, Pete, not 'motherfucker' – Millennium.

'I'll say this for David,' admits Jenny, grudgingly, 'he might disappear up his own arse sometimes, but he knows how to organise a holiday'. Perhaps too well: within a few hours David has organised rotas for cooking, washing-up, shopping and cleaning. The others start to get a little restless under this tyrannical regime.

For all three couples, it's a chance to reassess their relationships and look to the future; after all, there's a new mill... century just round the corner, and there are a lot of decisions to be made. For Adam and Rachel, the future seems rosy; he's recovered from his operation, they've put the whole Kris business behind them and they've realised that, come what may, they're meant for each other. And to cement the fact, they spend most of the weekend having noisy sex in their bedroom.

Pete and Jenny, who are separated from the other bedrooms by paper-thin walls, are feeling less certain about their relationship. They're back together in

Cold Facts

ⓖ Cold Feet's first major location shoot was on Lindisfarne – the perfect setting for a reflective New Year. Interiors, however, were shot at Hoghton Tower, near Preston.

ⓖ John Thomson gave himself a black eye when pulling up the anchor on the boat. Given Thomson's reputation as a practical joker, everyone on the crew thought it was a make-up stunt, and he got very little sympathy.

The perfect spot to see in the new millennium.

theory, but neither of them knows exactly what that means. Jenny's certainly not ready to resume sexual relations with Pete, despite the noisy encouragement coming from both adjacent bedrooms. But at least little Adam has his Dad back, and Jenny begins to realise that, for all his faults, Pete is really the man she loves. But can they put the past behind them?

David and Karen are having a wonderful time; they seem to have reached a new level of understanding, and once again they've been talking about enlarging their family. Karen's not too keen to discuss it: she's too busy throwing up in the mornings...

Adam and Pete, chafing under David's control-mania, sneak off in the boat for a pint on the mainland. They're away from home, away from their women – it's a chance for a rare serious talk. Pete confesses that he's actually jealous of Adam

In the middle of nowhere with just a few pizzas and a box of fireworks for company.

for having had cancer; he lost a testicle, but he got Rachel back. Pete wishes he could have a near-death experience in order to sort things out between him and Jenny. 'Be careful what you wish for,' advises Adam.

But wishes have a way of coming true all too quickly, and on their way back to the castle, laden down with pizza boxes (it was, after all, their turn to cook), the engine on the boat conks out and they're left stranded, terrified of drifting out into the open sea. Back at the castle, the others realise that Adam and Pete have disappeared, and mount a full-scale search. Beacons are lit, car headlamps illuminated... and finally the anxious seekers catch sight of a tiny spark out to sea. Adam is waving a lighted rag in the air to attract attention. Then, as it starts to burn his hand, he panics and drops it – straight on to a box of fireworks that David had bought to celebrate the New Year. Fearful for their lives, Pete and Adam jump overboard, only to find they're standing in two inches of water.

They return to dry land to a mixed reception. Rachel is overjoyed to have Adam back in her arms, safe and sound. Jenny, on the other hand, is furious with Pete for having put his life in danger; not, of course, because she really loves him, but because she doesn't want their child to grow up without a father. They row late into the night, overheard by their neighbours.

The countdown to midnight begins, somewhat hampered by the fact that Ramona has taken the batteries out of Pete's millennium clock for her Walkman. And as the old century wears away, a few home truths emerge. Pete and David have a blazing row, then make it up and cement their friendship. Adam proposes once again to Rachel, and they agree to go on holiday to Bali and see if they're in the mood to get married on the beach. Karen tells David that he's going to be a father again.

And so, unsure of exactly when the new century begins, our heroes sit out on the beach and wait for the dawn, wondering exactly what 2000 will bring to each of them.

Jenny's Other Men

Robert (Ben Miles)

Invited round to David and Karen's to make up the numbers at a dinner party, Jenny is surprised to meet a rich, attractive young businessman who clearly finds her very attractive. Robert's a pretty tasty proposition himself, not least because he soon develops some very good habits (sending Jenny huge amounts of flowers, taking her out for expensive meals, weekends in New York). A flirtation turns into an affair, and Robert becomes a fixture. The rest of the gang aren't best pleased; their loyalty will always be to Pete, and Robert's made to feel like a leper. Despite his best efforts  to be supportive to Jenny, and to accommodate her son, Robert finds the relationship difficult. Jenny is demanding and dogmatic, and eventually he starts to look elsewhere. After a few acrimonious scenes, Jenny and Robert part for good, and he takes his millions elsewhere.

Owen Claibourne (Norman Cooley)

The owner of the small but chic chain of hotels for which Jenny is working in the fourth series, Owen turns out to be an astute judge of character and whisks Jenny off for a job in New York. It's the chance she's been waiting for - at last someone has recognised her potential and given her a chance. But it all goes sour when Jenny and Owen end up having an affair, and she gets pregnant. Owen doesn't want to know, and Jenny returns to Manchester broke, unemployed and alone.

Ramona's Other Men

Javier (Javier Llamas)
We hear a lot about Ramona's famous Spanish boyfriend Javier, but we don't see a great deal of him, except in furious arguments. From what little we know, it seems that Javier's a good match for Ramona, in temperament at least. But Ramona's not prepared to be a good Spanish housewife, and soon poor Javier gets a final Adios.

Lee (Richard Armitage)
Long after her relationship with Pete, Ramona finally gets another bite at the cherry when she meets an attractive young instructor at the health club. Lee is a bit of a ladies' man, and at first Ramona is put off by his flirty ways - but he's persistent, and, after stringing him along a bit, she finally lets him have his wicked way with her. But the relationship is doomed; Lee, it turns out, has a bit of a past with Jo, which flares up again during a drunken marketing conference. Ramona finds out, and Lee is history.

'I hate you. I hope your plane crashes and you drown. Or get eaten by sharks. Whichever is more painful.'

Ramona wishes Javier a happy holiday

Chris Truelove

(PRODUCTION DESIGNER)

Cold Feet was set in a very specific place and time — the newly-affluent, newly-stylish, turn-of-the-century Manchester. 'Theres no way we could have made the show ten years ago,' says production designer Chris Truelove, 'at least not in Manchester. There just weren't the locations. The city has undergone such a massive regeneration in the last decade that it's unrecognisable as the place it once was. I think we were among the first people to show the new Manchester, and we had a part to play in putting it on the map as a good place to be.'

The city centre, in particular, was swarming with new bars, clubs and restaurants when *Cold Feet* started in 1997. '*Cold Feet* has always featured a lot of eating and drinking and socialising, and I was worried at first that we'd be scratching around to find attractive locations. But in the late 90's there was explosion of new venues in the centre; old buildings were being converted, and done up quite stylishly, and it seemed natural that our characters would gravitate towards new, fashionable places. Old offices and banks were being converted into bars and clubs, and the area round the canal was suddenly full of brand-new buildings. We were never short of choice. These places go quickly out of fashion, but they're always replaced by new ones. It was a time of rapid growth, certainly in Manchester, and the quick turnover of bars and restaurants is a sure symptom of that. We came back again and again to a few old favourites — Stocks, behind Marks and Spencer, for instance, and Bar 38 — but usually we just found the new, trendy place in town and went for that.'

Most of the time, the *Cold Feet*

> **'...it seemed natural that our characters would gravitate towards new, fashionable places.'**

gang is seen in domestic or social environments, but we also see into their working lives — and this set different challenges for Truelove and the design team. 'If you're shooting in a normal office, it can look quite claustrophobic on screen, and that was not the impression we wanted to give. So we were always looking for offices that had a lot of space: long rooms, glass partitions, anything that allowed the directors to use long lenses and get interesting shots. We only filmed in new buildings or new conversions; we wanted to convey the fact that Manchester was in the middle of an economic boom. So you'll see a lot of floor-to-ceiling glass partitions, a lot of beautiful atriums with marble walls and glass lifts. It was all about giving a sense of space and light – and there had to be room to fit a camera crew in there without knocking down walls.'

For the domestic exteriors, Truelove strove for authenticity, particularly in his choice of location. 'I knew immediately that Karen would live in Bowdon, an affluent suburb to the south-west of the city,' he says. 'They've got cash, and that's where prosperous Mancunians tend to live. It's full of solicitors, company directors, accountants and, of course, management consultants. Bowdon is full of large detached houses with gardens; it's very clean and well-kept, if a little bit boring. We located the others in Didsbury, which is closer to the city centre, and a bit less expensive, but very trendy and desirable. It's characterised by red brick Victorian semis and terraces, most of which have been converted.

The population is younger and a bit more fashionable, but it's by no means an inner-city environment. It's a nice place to live – it's the area that the *Cold Feet* characters would aspire towards.'

Filming around real buildings brings its own challenges and, over five years, the *Cold Feet* crew have had to deal with their fair share. 'When you're looking for a location, you just drive around the area until you find something that seems right. Then you knock on doors, and you sit down with the people and tell them what you want to do. You agree a fee,

'...people don't always want us back a second time.'

and then you try to be as careful as you can. Most people are up for it the first time round, but then they realise what a crew of 48 people tramping in and out of your house on a wet day can actually do. However careful we are, we're going to make a mess of a domestic interior. Sometimes we have to move people out of their own homes while we're shooting and put them up in hotels, which is expensive. And we always have to redecorate and make good any damage. So you can understand that people don't always want us back a second time. At first they're excited, they phone up their friends and families and tell them that their house is going to be on TV. After that, they can cool off pretty quickly.'

Such changes of heart have forced Truelove and his team to do some quick thinking. 'Adam and Rachel's house was the same property throughout all five series,' says Truelove, 'but we had to change the others. Pete and Jenny started off in

'Adam and Rachel's house was the same property throughout all five series.'

one house, then we had to move a few doors up the road, but that wasn't very satisfactory. By that time, though, the people who lived in the original house had moved, and we were able to negotiate with the new residents and go back. David and Karen's house was the hardest. We didn't have problems with the people who lived there – it was their neighbours in the cul-de-sac who didn't like the lights and the wagons and the noise. So we had to move to a completely different area, and then shoot the house in such a way as to minimise the change. Of course there's a certain amount that you can do by dressing up an exterior to disguise it, but eagle-eyed

viewers will realise that the Marsden's moved house without ever actually moving house.'

All the domestic exteriors are shot on location; the interiors, however, are entirely studio-bound. The sets have lasted, with additions and makeovers, through five series, moving from one studio to another. 'As soon as you've found your exterior,' says Truelove, 'you can start designing an interior to match it. My principle was always to create as much space as I could. I had rooms opening on to each other; I knocked down walls and tried to be open-plan. Like all the design in *Cold Feet*, the interiors were realistic but a little bit heightened. The rooms were four or five feet longer than they would be in a real Didsbury house, but that allows the directors to get a greater variety of shots and it just adds to the sense of style. It's like real life, but a bit better. The great thing about building interiors in the studio is that you can knock down walls or add extensions without bothering people. So when it came to a new series, if I wanted to tart something up a bit I could just stick on a conservatory or something. It's much easier.'

Again, Truelove tried to reflect the social standing of the characters in the interiors he created for them. 'Karen and David's house is a very affluent space; you can tell as soon as you look at it that these people have money. It's open plan, so its quite modern and stylish, but it's filled with very traditional, good-quality furniture. I think that says quite a lot about the Marsdens; they're trying to be fashionable, but they're very rooted in tradition. Adam and Rachel are much more the modern couple; they've got less money, but more adventurous taste. They've got wooden flooring, the type of stuff you can buy in packs and put down yourself, and they've got good, affordable modern furniture, a step or two up from Ikea. Their house is open plan, but a bit smaller than Karen and Davids. They've decorated in much more modern colours.'

'Pete and Jenny are at the other end of the scale. They're not poor, but they're less stylish than Adam and Rachel. Their's is a homely, cluttered interior, with a mix of furniture that they've been given by parents or bought second hand. It's a bit scruffy, but it has its own style that expresses the personality of the people living there. It's a sort of accidental style; Pete and Jenny are much less design-led than Adam and Rachel.'

The interiors have been erected for each new series, then taken down and put into storage in Granada's giant warehouses. Between the last two series, large parts were left up to serve as basic sets for other Granada productions, including The Grimleys and My Beautiful Son. 'Every time we start *Cold Feet* there's a lot of rebuilding and refurnishing to be done,' says Truelove. 'A lot of the props are hired from London, and you can't always get the exact same things back, so bits and pieces change from one series to another. Overall, though, we tried to recreate the same atmosphere each time. There were no radical changes in any of the interiors; nobody did a complete home makeover.'

But the *Cold Feet* sets have been rebuilt for the last time; at the end of the fifth series they were dismantled for good. 'We broke them all up and put them into seven or eight 40-foot lorries, which took them away for

'In a way I wish we'd been able to have a big bonfire and see them all go up in flames.'

landfill. It was very sad; that was a big part of my life. But there's nowhere to store sets of that size, so you have to destroy them. In a way I wish we'd been able to have a big bonfire and see them all go up in flames.'

And that, more than anything else, proves that the fifth series of *Cold Feet* really is the last.

David Marsden

(ROBERT BATHURST)

It takes time to get to know David. On first acquaintance, he seems a bit of a bore: pompous, shifty and cold. But that's not the real David. Underneath the typical management consultant exterior, there beats a heart of pure gold. Like all his friends, David makes mistakes, he allows his appetites to run away with him, he lies and cheats – but he does learn from his mistakes, and he genuinely tries to make up for anything he does wrong. It's his misfortune that he married a woman who is quick to anger and slow – very, very slow – to forgive.

More than anyone else in the show, David is a product of his background. He comes from a very posh family who packed him off to boarding school as soon as possible, and as a result he is very good at making superficial, professional friendships but doesn't have much of a clue when it comes to real intimacy. Matters were not helped by the fact that his parents seemed always to push him while indulging his ne'er-do-well younger brother, the black sheep of the family who only had to come crawling home with outstretched hand to get help and support. David, the first-born, always had to prove himself, and never got the kind of positive affirmation that he so desperately craved. Of course, his parents adored him – but they couldn't show it. It seemed like a frigid family, but there was plenty of emotion under the surface, struggling to find expression. David's parents failed to show their son how much they loved him; David himself is learning how to deal better with those same problems.

> **'They make some very underrated wines, the Bulgarians. Though this isn't one of them'**
>
> DAVID MARSDEN

And that isnt' the only legacy from David's past. As he discovers in therapy, his parents' marriage was almost destroyed by his father's adultery with his own sister-in-law. David's mother knew all about it, and kept the marriage going for the sake of the children – but any love between his parents was killed by this affair. And so David alternated between boarding school and a home life fraught with suppressed emotions. It's not a good start in life.

When we first meet him, David is almost the villain of the piece. He's unsympathetic to Karen's situation as a mother and housewife, he's content to go out to work and expects his meal to be on the table when he comes home. He sees himself as the breadwinner, and he believes that his wife should be content

For all his faults, David is the nicest of all the characters.

with the domestic sphere. In fairness, that's what he's been brought up to believe, and he's never come into contact with any progressive ideas that would challenge that. He was a young conservative at college, he was completely focused on getting a job, and the more radical movements of the 80s passed him by. So it comes as something of a shock to hear Karen demanding a nanny and wanting to go back to work. David's resistant at first. But sooner or later he gets the hang of it, and realises that it's good for his marriage and, ultimately, good for him.

And so it goes throughout David's life. He's resistant to anything that upsets the status quo, but usually comes to accept it through a mixture of genuine understanding and cynical self-interest. It's hard for him to resist his business instincts, and often this will bring him into conflict with his friends; right up to the end, he's trying to buy the house out from under Adam and Rachel's feet. But, unlike everyone else in the show, David usually ends up doing the right thing. In that instane, he stumps up the money to buy the house for his friends. It wasn't his first instinct, but he sees his mistake and rectifies it.

Money seems always to be David's prime interest, but what really interests him is what money can do for him. This can be something simple, like enjoying first class travel when everyone else is in economy. But more frequently, he likes money because he can do nice things for other people. He can take them on holiday, he can host parties, he can give presents. He doesn't expect much in return, and for that reason people tend to take advantage of him – David won't miss the money, they think, so they sometimes forget to be properly grateful. David regards this as bad manners, and is hurt by it. The happiest moment of his life is when he realises that, for once, his worst suspicions are wrong, and his friends have all clubbed together to buy him a motorbike for his 40th birthday.

David's relationship with Karen is the defining thing in his life. Really, those two were meant for each other, but their marriage is destroyed by frustration, bad timing and dishonesty. Karen likes to believe she's a free spirit, and thinks nothing of flirting with other men – but when David puts a foot wrong (well, several feet wrong) she retreats into the role of the injured wife and does everything in her power to punish him. David is truly repentant, learns from his mistake and wants to move on, but it's Karen who calls the shots. David's so decent, he lets her do it – and then, of course, the boot's on the other foot, and Karen's being unfaithful. Even then, he's ready to forgive – but life has other plans for David. Finally, the worm turns, and faced with the choice of an uncertain future with Robyn, or a familiar round of recriminations with Karen, he takes the braver option. Karen is left on her own, and David moves on. It's a fitting end to a journey from uptight, blinkered conservatism to battle-scarred experience.

Loves

♡ Money

♡ His children

♡ His Motorbike

♡ Karen

Hates

⊚ Dishonesty

⊚ Nightclubs

⊚ Karen's drinking

⊚ Mark

MIKE BULLEN ON David

I love David. He's a bit selfish and a bit insensitive, but his values are the strongest of them all. He's utterly reliable. You could ring him in the middle of the night if you needed help, and he'd be right round in a shot. He adores Karen, and will always love her whatever happens. Many women found David a complete prat until the fourth series, and then they began to understand him. There was that moment when we saw him flying back from Australia alone, utterly defeated, in tears... that was the big turning point. He's travelled the most of any of the characters. He started off as a stereotype and ended up as a real person. Cut him and he'll bleed. David makes mistakes, but he learns from them — and not all the characters can say that.

David's best just isn't good enough for Karen, and with Mark on the scene, it was never going to be.

Robert Bathurst

(David Marsden)

Robert Bathurst was convinced he was wrong for the role of David. 'When I went up for the audition I was doing Aphra Behn's *The Rover* at the Salisbury Playhouse, I was all bearded and shaggy and not at all like a smooth management consultant. But Christine Langan had seen me in *Joking Apart*, and in a series of staged sitcom pilots at the Riverside Studios in Hammersmith, so obviously she thought there was something there that she wanted. I went to the audition and did the meeting scene, when David gets conned by Karen into getting a nanny. I didn't feel at all right for the part. I thought they needed someone a lot shinier and flashier than me; someone who was really like that superficial yuppie character that Mike had initially written. When I got the part, I just approached it like any other job: I did it as well as I could, and that was that. It was never described to us as a series; it was just a 50-minute play.'

Bathurst was, at first, sceptical about *Cold Feet*'s chances of becoming a series. 'I'd been in two series of *Joking Apart*, and then that got dropped; it was at a time when ideas were coming up and just being squandered on television. Nobody would commit to anything. The morning after the pilot of *Cold Feet* was broadcast, I was pretty philosophical; it was a ratings disaster and a complete critical non-event. People were still talking about getting a commission, but I just said "I'll believe it when I see it". The good news was a long time coming - and even now I find it hard to believe that it's really been a success. I expect I'll look back in two years and think "Oh yes, that was rather good, wasn't it?"'

The show's success, according to Bathurst, was due to the fact that 'Mike Bullen allowed the characters to grow up. When *Cold Feet* started, it was trying to be young and funky. Now the characters are all a few years further on with more of life's baggage, the show has had to mature with them. Not all shows do that, particularly sitcoms; there's a danger that the characters get trapped in aspic and can never move on, so you end up with ageing actors playing characters who never grow old. But *Cold Feet* was never a sitcom. In fact it's never been anything: it doesn't fit anywhere. I think of it as a play in 33 acts. It's just a disparate group of people rubbing along together. We've covered a lot of issues, but the issues never intrude on the essence of the show. In its purest form, *Cold Feet* isn't 'about' anything at all. There are no 'isms'. It's less about events than people's reaction to events. It's all in the characters rather than the plot. When David had his affair, what was interesting was the fall-out rather than the affair itself. It was the deception, the guilt and the recrimination rather than the actual affair, which was neither interesting nor remarkable. *Cold Feet* was never a narrative as such; it's something much more complicated than that.'

The character of David perfectly embodies the way in which *Cold Feet* found depths where other shows presented only stereotypes. 'You'd think that David would always be rather shallow, and that's certainly how he started out. He was sexist, money-grubbing and incredibly dense. But then he changed, or at least our perceptions of him changed, because we got to

The boys

know him. That's why I like Mike's writing: there are no rules for the characters, they can develop and change as life affects them. He allows for human complications. Characters have the freedom to act out of character. That's very rare in TV drama. If you look at most soaps, you can see that the characters are restricted by a rigid definition of who and what they are, and if they step outside of that it doesn't ring true. In *Cold Feet*, the characters are just as fluid as people are in real life. There's no great secret to it; it's just good writing.'

In between series of *Cold Feet*, Bathurst has worked in a wide variety of different productions. At first he stuck to theatre, then, as the offers picked up, moved almost entirely into television. 'I get offered a lot of variations on the theme of David, and I try to avoid them. I got sent a script recently that was such an obvious rewrite of that character, it made my heart sink. But fortunately there is plenty of variety out there. In the last break I did *White Teeth* and *The Secret* - two very different roles in two very different dramas. *Cold Feet* has been good for all of us in that sense: we've got the opportunity to pick and choose from a wide range of offers. I want to take the work that interests me; there's no point in doing endless retreads of the same thing, because in two years time I'd be unemployable.'

Bathurst's first project after filming the final series of *Cold Feet* was My Dad's the Prime Minister, a family drama written by Ian Hislop and Nick Newman, with Bathurst as the PM. After that he will be back on the stage in the West End in Chekhov's *The Three Sisters*. 'But at the moment all I can think of is the holiday at the end of it all. Letting go of *Cold Feet* is very hard, so I'm glad I had a job to go straight into, but we all need a break. The last series has been very hard work, not least because it seems to be open season on us in the press at the moment, which puts a lot of silly pressures on you. But that will pass, and we'll get on with our lives. I'm sure that the cast of *Cold Feet* will continue to see each other; we've been working together for so long, you don't just cut yourself off from people like that.'

Ramona

(JACEY SALLES)

Ramona starts out as little more than a supporting artist – the stereotypical Spanish nanny who mangles the English tongue and spends her whole time on the phone to her family in Spain. But it soon emerges that there's more to her than that. She's great with Josh, giving him the attention that neither David nor Karen seems able to supply. And she's a breath of fresh air in the Marsden household, at least when she can get a word in edgeways. She's a lot more perceptive than her broken English would suggest – and, as Ramona becomes more confident in the language, it emerges that she's an acute observer of the domestic dramas of the Marsdens' marriage.

> **'I spy on him. And I good. My grandfather, he an informer for Franco.'**
>
> Ramona keeps an eye on Lee

Ramona likes to think of herself as a good catholic girl who would never have sex before marriage, but if that's the case it's wearing off quickly. She's delighted when Pete is attracted to her, and, while their relationship never gets much further than kisses and salsa classes, it's clear that Ramona is a good catch for any man that can get her. That turns out not to be the hapless Javier, who gets little more than the sharp side of Ramona's tongue and is eventually banished to the outer darkness. After a brief stint as a lap dancer in a West End club, Ramona settles down in her romantic life with Lee, the trainer from David and Karen's health club, and starts to plan her married life. Unfortunately for her, Lee's not the marrying kind – and, at the end of the show, Ramona and Karen are facing a future as two single women together.

Ramona, despite her impulsive moments, is a good woman to have around in a crisis. She's understanding, practical and forgiving – which is a great deal more than her employers can say. She realises that David's repentance after

Loves
- ♡ Josh and the twins
- ♡ Salsa
- ♡ Evenings off
- ♡ David's repentance

Hates
- ☺ Javier
- ☺ The neighbours
- ☺ Karen's drinking
- ☺ Lee's infidelity

Ramona needs more money – gambling on horses is not the best way to get it.

his affair with Jessica is real, and she urges Karen to swallow her pride, if only for the sake of the children. And, as Karen and David's marriage hits the rocks, Ramona tries to rescue Karen from incipient alcoholism and to comfort Josh, who is deeply upset by his parents' constant rowing. In the end it's too much for her, and she accepts a tempting offer from the Marsdens' two-timing neighbours, and goes to work for them. It doesn't last – they're the employers from hell, and soon Ramona is back with her beloved Josh.

Ramona is really one of the most stable, self-determined characters in the cast, and we can only hope that, after she's got over Lee, she'll find a man to make her happy and start a family of her own. She's wasted as a nanny.

Jacey Salles

(Ramona)

Jacey Salles was originally signed up for little more than a bit part. 'David and Karen got a nanny at the beginning of the first series, and I was contracted for two episodes. After that I assumed they'd get rid of Ramona and hire a Polish nanny or something, and just keep changing them. But then I was told that more lines were being written for me, and that character started to grow.'

Jacey had been doing bits and pieces of acting work as well as running her own restaurant in the West End of London, Café Mania (now called Squat and Gobble). 'There were always a lot of production people in there, and I was forever hassling for a part. Eventually I got a small piece playing a Spanish diva in a film that Andy Harries and Christine Langan were working on, and that's how they knew about me for *Cold Feet*. And now I tend to get every Spanish role that's going.'

It's not entirely acting: Jacey's father is Spanish, her mother English, and she's fluent in both languages. 'What they wanted for *Cold Feet* was someone who was the complete antithesis to the British way of life. Karen and David are quiet and repressed; Ramona is loud and passionate. In the audition I had a loud argument with an imaginary boyfriend on the telephone, in Spanish, and did a bit of comic bastardisation of the English language, and I got the part. At first I only had a couple of lines, and I just thought of *Cold Feet* as a little, quick job that I'd do before moving on to something else. But somehow Ramona became part of the show. At first she was a good foil for David; he mocked her language difficulties, she wound him up by always using the telephone. Those funny bits became more and more frequent and then I got signed up for the second series.'

Gradually Ramona became an indispensable part of the team – and in the third series she was given her first major storyline with one of the principal characters. 'The second series was a bit strange and transitional for me. There were a lot more moments, but there were long gaps in between. It was a bit like sitting in the dole office waiting for your number to come up. But the reaction from the public was always positive, and the producers realised that they could turn Ramona into a bigger character. So in the third series she got together with Pete, and people loved it. Everyone had something to say about it! Suddenly I was very recognisable. Women with kids, especially, loved the character. They'd stop and tell me how much they enjoyed it, and they loved the way Ramona got things wrong all the time. I had to start watching my step. I'd get people coming up to me in cafes, or in the gym, even in the showers, and saying 'You're Ramona, aren't you?'. I realised I couldn't be grumpy or snappy in public any more.'

In between series of *Cold Feet*, Jacey has fitted in a good deal of work –

everything from a film with Jeremy Northam (*The Misadventures of Margaret*) to
panto in Rickmansworth, playing the Wicked Queen in *Snow White*. 'I take what
I can, but I've got a baby so I can't work full time. Everyone on *Cold Feet* has kids.
Helen and I would bring our children on to set. It's difficult being a full-time
actress and a full-time mother. To be honest, *Cold Feet* has been really hard work.
I think of the show as a very high-maintenance, 35-year-old woman, a sort of
wonderful diva. She needs all the make-up and the right lighting, but she does a
great job. Making the show is a slog; it's afterwards that I enjoy it, when I look
back and think of how much fun we had. It's strange to think that it's really over
now. Maybe one day it will come back – Adam will wake up from a dream, and
Rachel will step out of the shower. If *Only Fools and Horses* can go on for 100
years, why not *Cold Feet*?'

Series 3

12 Nov – 31 Dec 2000 ⓖ 8 episodes

It's taken them a long time, but Adam and Rachel are finally ready to **tie the knot**. Or are they? Much of series three is taken up with a classic case of cold feet as the star-crossed **lovers** move inevitably towards **marriage**. Are they doing it for the right reasons? Can they ever put the past behind them? Everyone has a great deal to say about the subject, at least behind each other's back... But finally, after much **soul-searching**, the wedding goes ahead, a **happy** ending to the series.

But Adam and Rachel aren't facing a future without problems. Throughout the entire series, they're trying to have children. An early **pregnancy** turns out to be a false alarm, and from then on it's a tiring, expensive business of **fertility** treatments. And then Rachel discovers that she's **infertile**, possibly as a result of the abortion. Well, they'll just embrace a childless future – if, that is, Adam can keep his hands off his former girlfriends. Adam's **stag night** in Portrush is nearly memorable for all the wrong reasons...

Pete and Jenny have decided to call it a day, and for the whole of series three they're seeing other people. Jenny's got Robert, the dot com **millionaire**; Pete tries his luck with Ramona and Emma. But nobody seems to come up to scratch, and while the Gifford vs Gifford **divorce** grinds into action both Pete and Jenny wonder if they're doing the right thing.

Karen and David aren't having much more luck. He's started an **affair** — and, although it takes Karen the entire series to find out, it's more than their marriage can stand.

Series 3

Episode 1

New twin sisters and a drunken granny for Josh ... Pete moves back in as Jenny's lodger ... Jenny meets a very eligible bachelor ... Is Rachel pregnant?

Karen comes home from the hospital with a big surprise: not just one new baby sister for Josh, but two. Josh is less than thrilled to have twins competing for his parents' attention, and lets his feelings be known in little ways – like balancing an iron above their cot, for instance.

As if the Marsdens didn't have enough problems, Karen's mother Heather arrives hotfoot from the Costa del Sol, and immediately starts treating the house like a hotel. It's not just her abrasive manner that gets on David's nerves; it's the fact that she's drinking like a fish. Karen realises that something's wrong.

Rachel and Adam get back from a holiday in Mauritius to find Pete stretched out stark naked on their sofa, surrounded by empty beer cans and pizza cartons. He's been staying in the spare room, and the entire house is filthy ('I hope you haven't got skid marks on the sofa, Pete,' says Rachel). Pete's desperate; he has nowhere else to go, but even Adam agrees that it's impossible to have him staying any longer. And so he goes back to the marital home – as Jenny's lodger.

Adam and Rachel don't have peace for long, though; Karen and David have decided it would be a good idea if Josh came to stay with them for a few days, as a special holiday treat, while the twins settle in. It's not quite what Adam and Rachel had planned, but before too long they find that they rather enjoy having a mischievous four-year-old around the house – even if he does interrupt their sex life and cause havoc in the car wash.

Karen and David are planning a dinner party to entertain a couple of clients of David's: Felix Bishop, a middle-aged venture capitalist, and Robert Brown, an attractive young internet millionaire.

Double Trouble

⑥ Karen and David's twin daughters were played by the Bateson triplets, who were found thanks to the good offices of the Bolton Health Authority.

⑥ Three babies made life much easier than two, allowing one to rest while the others worked. This happy arrangement only worked for one series though – after that it became too apparent that one of the triplets was a boy!

David and Karen have their hands
full with the twins.

Suddenly they find themselves one woman short, and so Karen calls Jenny to
stand in at the last moment. She's happy to oblige; the alternative was a TV
dinner with Pete, who's making himself very comfortable in his old home.

On arriving at the dinner party, Jenny assesses the guests. Felix, she decides,
is a 'borderline groper'. Heather is a lush. Robert, as a colleague of David's, is
'probably dickless'. When she learns that Robert is not only a millionaire but also
straight and single, she rapidly revises her opinion; could this be the flash new
boyfriend she's been fantasising about? He's certainly a far cry from no-hoper
Pete. Jenny's not the only one with her eye on a new man; Heather's getting on
famously with Felix. Karen's at a loss to explain her mother's flirtatious behaviour;
what would Dad think? 'I've left your father,' announces Heather, before swanning
out of the kitchen to rejoin Felix.

Pete's bored at home, and goes round to tell Adam and Rachel that he thinks
he and Jenny have a good chance of getting back together again; little does he
know that Jenny is, at that moment, having a tender moment with Porsche-
driving Robert. There's little time to comment on Pete's announcement, though;
Adam discovers that Josh has shaved himself bald in the bathroom. A little

'She looks like a cheap tart.
I'm sorry. I take back cheap.'

David on Karen's mother

emergency hairdressing only makes matters worse, and they're obliged to return the child to his parents wearing a brand new woolly hat.

Jenny's flirtation with Robert turns into something more serious when he tracks her down at her awful, dead-end office job and asks her if she'll go out for lunch. She accepts the invitation; she's just got the sack anyway. Meanwhile Pete is shopping for a special celebration meal; it's his and Jenny's anniversary, and he wants to show her how much he appreciates being back in the house. His romantic gesture backfires badly when Jenny receives a huge bouquet of flowers – not from Pete, but from Robert.

Adam and Rachel's house is very quiet now that Josh has left, and they realise that they both enjoyed having a kid around the place. 'I'm glad you've said that,' says Rachel, 'because you know our special friend, that comes to stay every now and then?' 'Pete?' says Adam, mystified. 'No. My period. It's late.'

Jenny is told she's unemployable. Like she cares!

Episode 2 (written by David Nicholls)

Has Jenny found a new man?... Will Pete find a new home?...
What has prompted David's sudden interest in politics?...
Will Adam and Rachel ever have a baby?

Things aren't going well for Pete and Jenny since the split. She's wasting her time in a series of dead-end jobs, fantasising about romance and riches, while he's homeless and, seemingly, friendless. Adam and Rachel have other things to think about, and the last thing they need is Pete sleeping on their sofa. At least there's some light at the end of the tunnel for Jenny: she's getting phonecalls from Robert, who seems keen. She's not sure if she's ready to get involved this soon, but anything has got to be better than the tedium of the life she's currently living. And when he sends her flowers – not just a bunch, not just a bouquet, but

Jenny's fantasy life is worryingly vivid.

David and Karen, long before we knew them.

(top) Pete and Jenny in happier, less complicated days.
(bottom) Adam and Rachel: True love never dies.

(top) Karen's hopes for an affair with Alexander Welch came to nothing.
(bottom) But with Mark, things got a lot more serious.

(top) Surprising even himself, David finally gave in to Jessica's charms.
(bottom) But he found happiness with Robyn.

(top) If Adam and Pete weren't best friends who knows what could have happened between him and Jenny.

(bottom) And as for Robert – Jenny's friends proved too much for him.

(top) Pete and Ramona had a brief fling.
(bottom) But the arrival of Jo seemed to give Pete the happy ending he craved.

Friends and Lovers

(top) Rachel's ex-husband, the perfect Kris, caused havoc when he reappeared.
(bottom) So did Adam's first love Jane, but at least she didn't have to be paid off!

Things aren't always what they seem...
(top) Take Karen and Pete for example
(bottom) Or Rachel in bed with a mystery man.

enough flowers to cover the whole of her house – Jenny begins to think that maybe Robert's a pretty attractive proposition.

Adam's excited about Rachel's late period; so excited that he can't stand still, can't listen to anyone else's problems, and certainly hasn't got time to listen to Pete. That leads to a flare-up between them, in which Pete accuses Adam of alienating Jenny and basically ruining his life. Pete realises he's gone too far, and sneaks out of the house before he can face Adam in the morning. But Adam's good mood is quickly deflated too; Rachel's pregnancy turns out to be a false alarm. Both put on a brave face, and toast 'a near miss', but the strain is beginning to tell as both of them wonder whether they'll ever be able to conceive.

Karen is understandably peeved when David appears to be throwing her mother Heather at his business associate, Felix. David can only see the professional advantages of such a relationship; Karen, however, is more concerned about her father, who's back in Spain and knows nothing of all this.

A chance visitor to the Marsdens' household throws their carefully-ordered life into a spin. Jessica represents the local residents' association, and she's looking for support for a petition to stop the council developing a new shopping mall on the site of the existing park and playground. David is sceptical, but, goaded by Karen, he agrees to go along to the meeting and to fight for a facility that his son uses constantly. At first he's nothing but disruptive, but when he recognises that the campaign poses a challenge to his management skills he jumps at the bait, and is soon organising the petition and treating everyone like an employee. His new-found enthusiasm may have something to do with the fact that he finds Jessica undeniably attractive... After the meeting he comes home full of beans, and announces that he may even join the Labour Party – which comes as some surprise to Karen, as the only organisation David's ever joined before is the RAC. Little does she know that this sudden interest has very little to do with party politics.

Pete's looking for a flat – a demoralising experience that not only makes him realise how old he's got, but also reminds him of happier times when he and Jenny took their first rented accommodation together. After a few rejections, he finds a house-share with Matthew, a fellow-divorcé, and braces himself for a new life as a single man. Adam and Rachel come round to settle Pete to his new home, and immediately notice that his new landlord is gay. Pete can't believe it – and then, when he realises that they're right, he loses his temper and accuses them of being smug, always laughing at him, thinking of him as nothing more than a sad fat bastard who lives with a lonely old queen. Unfortunately for Pete,

Rock-bottom. Pete searches desperately
for a place to live.

Robert is not put off by Jenny's choice of restaurant.

Matthew overhears the last part of this tirade.

Robert's in hot pursuit of Jenny. He follows up the forest of flowers with phone calls, dinner invitations, the full number. It's impossible for Jenny to resist, and eventually she agrees to a dinner date – at the restaurant of her choice. This turns out to be an eat-as-much-as-you-like curry house, where you get after-dinner mints and a carnation for the lady – a long way from the establishments favoured by super-rich Robert. But he has a good time, takes her home – and stays the night. Within a matter of days, he's asking her to come away with him to New York for the weekend. Jenny's always wanted to go – but first there's the little issue of childcare. It's Pete's turn to look after Adam for the weekend, but Pete's less than keen about allowing his wife to go off to Manhattan with a new man. It had always been Pete's dream to take her there, and it's a hard dream to let go of.

Adam and Rachel have been avoiding the issue of fertility so successfully that all their friends assume that they're the perfect modern couple. Beneath this chirpy exterior, however, all is far from well. Adam's feeling emasculated, Rachel fears that her failure to conceive may be related to her termination – and this anxiety and guilt is leading to regular rows. Finally they agree to seek treatment, and the doctor recommends intra-cytoplasmic sperm injection, a costly and painful process which will make the best use of the sperm Adam banked prior to his operation. But they agree that, in the meantime, they'll keep trying for a baby in the normal way, and have as much fun as possible doing so.

Pete apologises to Matthew, and a tentative friendship is born. And he relents on the babysitting issue, regretfully allowing Jenny to spread her wings and fly to America – without him.

Episode 3 <small>(written by David Nicholls)</small>

David's having a party... Karen's mother departs... Rachel undergoes a fertility 'procedure'... And who's that doing a salsa in Karen and David's living room?

There's sex in the air for all the characters at the start of this episode. Pete has a chance meeting in the park with Ramona; they're brought together when Josh dumps an ice-cream over little Adam's head. After such inauspicious beginnings, this ill-assorted pair find themselves chatting like old friends – and Pete finds himself suddenly keen to take his son to the park on a more regular basis.

Jenny, meanwhile, is rediscovering the joy of sex with Robert. Obviously the New York trip worked wonders, and now they're at it hammer and tongs the moment they have the house to themselves. There's only one fly in the ointment; none of Jenny's friends want to have anything to do with Robert, out of loyalty to Pete. Jenny's not the kind of girl to let something like that hold her back, but it's a big cloud on the horizon nevertheless.

As for David, he's teetering on the brink of an affair with Jessica. In his own mind, he's already an adulterer; he's dreamed of having sex with Jessica, he takes her out for drinks and flirts with her, and seems to be heading inexorably towards a foregone conclusion. Perhaps it's a mid-life crisis: after doing a 'Things You Should Have Done Before You're 30' quiz with Adam, David realises that he's missed out on all the fun things in life – and he's ten years older. His 40th birthday is fast approaching, and he's determined to enter his fifth decade with a spring in his step and a fire in his loins. And so he organises a party. Not a nice, respectable dinner party, but a big, noisy proper party with loud music, plenty of booze and, with a bit of luck, some snogging. And so he set about the guest list...

Rachel and Adam are thinking about sex for different reasons: they're still trying to conceive, and have turned up at the clinic for their first ICSI treatment. Rachel tries to relax as Adam's sperm is placed into her egg – but that's hard to do when the music on their chosen CD turns out to be Queen rather than Marvin Gaye. (Pete's been playing DJ again.) There's a one-in-five chance of the treatment working, but Adam and Rachel try hard to look on the bright side.

Heather continues to be a thorn in Karen's side. Not only is she drinking her out of house and home, but she's continuing her sleazy (thinks Karen) affair with Felix, and to cap it all she smacks Josh. Defiant, Heather swans off to her date

with Felix – only to return with her tail between her legs some hours later, confessing that it all went horribly wrong when she discovered that Felix had taken her to a swingers' party and expected her to join in the fun. This is enough to persuade Heather to put her problems behind her and return to Spain – and Karen's father. It's the best possible ending to a highly stressful episode.

David's 40th birthday party is looming – and to everyone's disgust, it's fancy dress. To add to the complication, David's decided not to invite Pete; he wants Jenny to come and have a good time, and he feels, rather uncharitably, that Pete will just throw cold water over the evening. Needless to say Pete finds out that he's not invited, but he has an ace up his sleeve. As the days tick by, he finds

Pete and Ramona perform a
perfect Salsa.

himself unexpectedly busy in the evenings with Ramona.

On the evening of the party, all the friends are getting ready in their ridiculous fancy dress costumes. Rachel's decided to go as King Kong; she's in a fragile emotional state because of the fertility treatment, and doesn't want anyone to talk to her. Adam's going as James Bond, while Jenny and Robert are coming as Princess Leia and John Travolta. David and Karen are Mad Max and Uma Thurman; Jessica turns up as Charlie Chaplin. 'Who's the little tramp?' asks Karen, in all innocence; a guilty David interprets this as a slur on the woman he's been intending to sleep with.

Finally, to everyone's astonishment, Pete and Ramona turn up as Zorro and Catherine Zeta Jones, and execute a perfect salsa on the dancefloor. They're the hit of the evening, and after their performance things start to go with a swing. David has an unplanned kiss with Jessica, while Jenny is forced to face up to her own feelings of jealousy when she sees Pete in the arms of another woman. At the end of the party, everyone drifts home, leaving David and Karen to reflect on a successful evening. Just one thing's troubling David: none of his friends bought him a present. Oh well, says Karen, not to worry; they're all very busy people.

The next morning, David staggers downstairs to get a cup of tea – and there, in the middle of the living room floor, is a brand new shiny Harley Davidson motorbike, a birthday present from his wife and all his friends. David roars off down the road, happy in the knowledge that life begins at 40.

King of the Road. Life begins at 40 for David.

Episode 4

David's reaching the point of no return with Jessica... But what about Karen and Miles?... Pete begins to explore alternative lifestyles... Adam proposes to Rachel — again.

Adam and Rachel's first attempt at ICSI was unsuccessful, and so they're obliged to go cap-in-hand to the bank for a loan of £4000 to try again. The bank manager seems far from sympathetic, but in the end the money comes through. It's a testing moment; wouldn't they be happier just forgetting about a family and using the money to go on a fantastic holiday? But in the end they decide that they have to try for a child, as it's what they both really want in life. The uncertainty continues.

Pete's relationship with Ramona is coming along nicely; they're dating regularly, they seem to have a lot in common, and she's even prepared to come and watch him play football. She's the only woman at the ground, though: the team that Pete's been roped into is his landlord Matthew's all-gay five-a-side, and Pete's in goal. The match goes well, and Pete saves the day – but a passionate congratulatory kiss from Ramona almost throws the match. It's okay, says Ramona, he's bisexual... And that seems to be enough for the rest of the lads. Pete finds he's very much at home with his new friends, and starts going out for drinks with them in Manchester's gay village.

Not long now... David's about to throw caution to the wind.

'You are the only person I know who phoned the police to complain about their own party.' Karen to David

David is getting more and more involved with Jessica. It's a strange attraction, a mixture of excitement over his campaign to save the playground, genuine physical arousal and a certain amount of forbidden fruit. The more he sees Jessica, the more he finds himself fantasising about sex with her – not to mention Karen's response if she found out he was having an affair.

Karen gets another surprise one morning when collecting the post; she finds Pete creeping down the stairs from Ramona's room, where he spent the night. Cool Karen doesn't miss a beat, and invites Pete to join them for breakfast; David is less cool about the affair, believing that it represents an unacceptable crossing of the line between 'upstairs' and 'downstairs'. Coming from a man who's teetering on the brink of adultery, this sounds like the very worst kind of hypocrisy. But Karen couldn't care less. She's hooked up with an old flame of hers from college, photographer Miles Brodie, and soon she's reliving her wild student days during their regular dates. Karen may be the perfect middle-class mother now, but she wasn't always thus: at college, she and Miles used to organise Socialist Workers' Party rallies, and would often have sex after a good riot. That kind of excitement is missing from her life now, and Karen's all too aware that she opted for the safer, less exciting, path with David.

Miles is back, resurrecting memories of Karen's lost youth.

But David's not as safe as Karen thinks. After a successful confrontation with the playground developers, in which he and Jessica make an unbeatable double-act, David finds himself with his tongue down Jessica's throat and his hands inside her clothes. It looks like the point of no return, but with heroic self-mastery David draws back from the brink and returns to his office as if nothing had happened – remembering, in the nick of time, to do up his flies.

Pete takes Adam for a drink to one of his new watering holes on Canal Street. Adam's shocked that it's a gay bar at first, but after a couple of pints he's wildly enthusing about Pete's new friends and is delighted to hear that one of them fancied him. This is not what Pete wants to hear; he's sick of Adam muscling in on his friends and his life. It seems that he's still not forgiven him for alienating Jenny's affections, and the cracks are beginning to show.

Adam may seem horribly insensitive to Pete's predicament, but he has troubles of his own. The fertility treatments aren't working, and a scan reveals that it's got nothing to do with the quality of Adam's sperm. The problem lies with Rachel; she has a condition known as Partial Ashermans, a result of her termination, which makes it almost impossible for her to conceive. The couple leave the clinic in a state of shock, and go their separate ways to seek solace with their friends.

Rachel runs to Karen, only to be confronted with the spectacle of a pet rabbit that's just given birth to six little bunnies. It's the last thing she needed to see, and Rachel breaks down – accidentally squashing one of the rabbits in the process. Adam goes to Jenny, and pours his heart out. For once, Adam's happy-go-lucky mask slips, and we see the depth of his confusion. 'When did we start making such a bollocks of our lives?' he asks Jenny, who has no answer for him.

Adam and Rachel meet up at home. Both have been doing a lot of thinking. She's decided that it's not fair to tie Adam down when they can never have a family, and so she offers him his freedom. His response is unexpected: he proposes marriage.

'A touch of clinging to the wreckage about it.'

Adam and Rachel's announcement does not impress Jenny

Episode 5

Who is Brenda Heeve?... David finally bows to the inevitable... Jenny and Robert are feeling the strain... Are Adam and Rachel doing the right thing?

With friends like these, who needs enemies? Adam and Rachel have rallied the gang for dinner at a Chinese restaurant so that they can break the good news about their engagement. Everyone smiles and offers their congratulations, but no sooner are Karen and Jenny alone in the loos than they're dissecting Rachel's motives for marriage, and deciding that infertility is a really bad reason for a wedding. Rachel remains in blissful ignorance: when she finds her two girlfriends she asks them outright for their opinion, and they tell her that, of course, it's a splendid idea and they're very happy for her.

Adam and Rachel's happiness is in marked contrast to the rest of the group. Jenny's brought Robert to dinner, and he's received with chilly politeness; Adam, in particular, refuses to be nice to him. The cracks in this fledgling romance are already beginning to show. Pete, meanwhile, admits that he's filling in the empty hours at Robert's house by playing around on the internet, discussing football with his pals in cyberspace. And David is obsessed by the idea of cheating on Karen; he can't stop thinking about Jessica, and what they could do together. He's almost convinced himself that he's already having an affair, while Karen's mind is all on Brodie. There's only one way that this situation is going to resolve itself.

A slip of the tongue on Jenny's part reveals to Rachel what public opinion really makes of her forthcoming wedding. Rachel returns home in contemplative mood, and tells Adam that perhaps they should settle for a long engagement. They can get married when it feels right... But when will it feel right?

Pete finally seems to have met someone new: a woman in the chatrooms under the name of Girlpower. His big mistake, of course, is to tell Adam about it – and Adam can't resist wading in to spoil things. He logs into the chat room using Girlpower's nickname, and proceeds to tell Pete all the things 'she' would like them to do when they finally meet. Pete's confused when, next time he chats to Girlpower, she denies all knowledge of this conversation. Perhaps she has a personality disorder, suggests Adam helpfully. Pete's none the wiser, little suspecting that his so-called best friend is trying to nip his new relationship in the bud.

Surprisingly, Karen and Jenny keep
their thoughts about Rachel's wedding
to themselves – for once!

David finally bows to the inevitable and takes Jessica to a hotel in the afternoon. We haven't seen him this nervous since his visit to Trixie the prostitute; this time, however, he does a lot more than talk. Jessica seems to take their sexual relationship in her stride; for David, it's a big deal, and he can't stop thinking about the damage he's doing to his marriage. Should he confess to Karen? His guilt haunts his every waking hour, while Karen seems to be completely oblivious. She's got other fish to fry; her rekindled friendship with Brodie brings back memories of intimate moments under the stage at a Rock Against Racism gig, when they had sex while the Stranglers were playing 'Peaches'. And there's much more to this than a mild flirtation: soon Karen is helping Brodie to set up an exhibition of his photographs.

After weeks of skirting around the issue, David and Jessica finally get it together.

'An intelligent, attractive, affectionate woman who's not that fussed.' What Pete likes about Emma

Her big mistake is to enlist the services of a newly-unemployed Jenny, who's just looking for a big project upon which to exercise her formidable powers of organisation. She can't wait to get her teeth into Brodie's exhibition – and she organises it to such an extent that first Karen, then Robert, then Brodie begin to wish that she'd never started. Jenny's control-freak tendencies are in full spate, and it's not doing her any good at all.

Pete's online relationship with Girlpower has gone a step further: he's got a real-time date, and has discovered that her real identity is Brenda Heeve, schoolteacher. She invites him to pick her up at work one afternoon – and so Pete turns up at the playground at the appointed time. He's met by two sassy schoolgirls with whom he trades the traditional playground insults ('your breath smells') until they take him into the classroom to meet Miss Heeve.

Could this be the beginning of a new romance for Pete? Well, probably not, as Brenda Heeve turns out to be a figment of the girls' imagination, an anagram of Ever Been Had?, invented as part of a project to demonstrate the power of the internet. Pete's been well and truly had, and tells Adam all about it. Adam thinks he'll have the last laugh – until Pete reveals that, after all that, he got a date with the real teacher, Emma.

Brodie's exhibition is a great success, thanks in no small part to Jenny's organisational skills, which may be incredibly irritating, but are undeniably effective. Realising that she's alienated Karen, Jenny swallows her pride and begs her friend to forgive her. And so the gang is reunited at the gallery, where Karen bids for one of the photographs, a beach scene in Mauritius, as an engagement present for Adam and Rachel.

It's all that Adam and Rachel need to set them off thinking about marriage again – and by the end of the episode they've decided that maybe a long engagement isn't such a good idea after all.

Homecoming

James Nesbitt lived around the Portrush area, where Adam's stag night was filmed, from the age of about 11. He was, among other things, a bingo caller.

Episode 6 (written by David Nicholls)

It's time to reveal some secrets...David tells one to Pete...
Jenny tells one to Rachel... Adam keeps one from Rachel...
What does the future hold for our six confused heroes?

Now that the date's been set for Adam and Rachel's wedding, the most important business in hand is the stag and hen nights. Adam's being whisked away to a mystery destination by his best man, who gets him as far as Manchester Airport without revealing the secret. They're going somewhere that begins with B, is all Pete will say. Barcelona? Berlin? Bilbao? No: it's Belfast, and just to make it extra special David's coming along for the ride. Adam's a little disappointed when he finds that all his other old friends, who have names like Ludders, Carsey, The Hawk and Bucket, can't make it — but a trip home is a trip home, and he's determined to savour this last weekend of freedom.

Rachel, predictably, has chosen what she wants to do for her hen weekend: she's booked the girls into Faversham Hall, a posh health spa, and is looking

'This, my friends, is where Adam Williams lost his virginity.'

'You've got to get drunk and snog a stranger on your hen night. It's the law.'

Jenny's none too pleased with Rachel's choice of hen night

forward to 48 hours of seaweed wraps, holistic massage and Alexander technique. Jenny and Karen are less than thrilled by the prospect of a hen night without booze, fags or men, but decide that it will do them good in any case.

Adam, Pete and David arrive in Belfast airport where they're met by their chauffeur for the weekend, a lugubrious Irishman named Roy, whose only real concern seems to be that they won't throw up on his soft covers. It's not an auspicious start, but Adam soon gets into the swing of things by showing his friends round some of the city's major historical landmarks – or at least the houses where all his girlfriends lived. Finally he takes them out to the Giants' Causeway, and shows them the bench where he lost his virginity to his first true love, Jane Fitzpatrick, the only woman he ever seriously considered marrying before Rachel. And there on the bench is the graffiti that marked that close encounter: ADAM W 4 JANE F 20/6/83 TRUE LUV. What went wrong? asks David. Well, Adam got off with another woman, of course, and that was the end of that. In reflective mood, Adam allows himself to be led off to a quayside pub for a drink with the boys, but he's dismayed to find that what was once a lively local seems to be dying on its feet. Then the doors open and there's... everybody! Pete's organised an entire stag party – and there among the guests is Jane Fitzpatrick.

Back in Faversham Hall, Jenny and Karen's resolve has melted away and they're already raiding the contents of their minibar. Rachel walks in and discovers them hitting the booze – and, to their great relief, decides to join in. Several drinks later, and someone suggests a game of Spin the Bottle. It starts off well enough, with Rachel belting out New York, New York while the others wear their pants on their heads and put on foolish clown make-up. But alcohol and truth games prove to be a dangerous combination, and Jenny accidentally reveals that she got off with Adam during her marriage to Pete. This is news to Rachel, who bursts into tears and announces that there won't be a wedding.

Oblivious to this drama across the water, Adam is thoroughly enjoying his stag party, and is particularly happy to catch up with the lovely Jane. She reminds him of their pact to meet up on New Year's Eve, 1999, and tells him that she was there at the old bench waiting for him but he didn't turn up... Adam's shocked, but Jane assures him it was just a joke. Determined to find out what her true feelings are, Adam takes Jane off for a walk as Roy the cabbie launches into another verse of Danny Boy.

While Adam's having his dangerous liaison with Jane, David confesses to Pete that he's been having an affair behind Karen's back. Pete's furious: he had an affair,

and look what it did to his marriage! He makes David promise to knock it on the head the moment he gets back to Manchester.

Jenny finds Rachel swimming alone in the hotel pool. She tries to explain to her that nothing really happened between her and Adam, that it was just a crush, a result of her unhappiness with Pete. Eventually Rachel is convinced, and they make friends again. The wedding's back on – but the hen night is over. The girls realise that there's only one place for them on this particular evening, and that's with their men. There's a flight to Belfast in a couple of hours, and so they check out of Faversham Hall and hotfoot it to the airport.

While Rachel is flying to meet him, Adam wakes up with a sore head – in Jane Fitzpatrick's bed. A kiss on the Giants' Causeway led to more – but how much more? Adam can't remember and, gentleman that he is, asks Jane outright if they had sex. No, they didn't, she tells him – you've nothing to regret. They part on a bitter note. Adam wants her to meet Rachel, to be friends with her – and this is not what Jane wanted to hear.

But the flight has landed, the girls turn up, and they find Adam wandering down the street. 'I know everything' says Rachel to her horrified fiancé. 'Everything?' says Adam. 'About me and Jane?' His Belfast accent saves him; Rachel thinks he says 'Jen'. 'Yes, I know everything, and I forgive you.' The danger has passed, and Rachel tells him how much she's looking forward to a life without secrets. Adam can only marvel at his lucky escape.

The friends gather on the beach as clouds of uncertainty gather over the future. Can Adam ever really be truthful with Rachel? Can David rescue his marriage from the abyss of adultery? And what does the future hold for Pete and Jenny? There seems to be a slight thawing in their relationship – but neither knows how to make the next step.

Episode 7 (written by David Nicholls)

Rachel's wedding plans spin out of control... Karen is arrested... Jessica dumps David... Robert dumps Jenny... Pete and Jenny get a divorce

The stag and hen nights are over, and, miraculously, the wedding is still on. All that remains now is to plan it – and that proves to be such a strain on Adam and Rachel's relationship that the wedding is nearly called off again. To start off with, they have very different ideas about scale. He'd like a small do with a couple of dozen close friends. She's thinking big, and her smallest guest list is 143, including all family members, whether they like them or not. This is going to be a long battle...

As usual, Adam takes his troubles to Pete. But Pete's in no mood to listen; despite Adam's internet meddling, he's dating Emma, the teacher that he met after the Girlpower episode. She's just what he wanted – 'an attractive, intelligent, affectionate woman who's not that fussed' – and she likes football! Finally Pete comes down off his cloud for long enough to take Adam shopping for an engagement ring – and David comes along as well, to make sure that Adam doesn't try and get away with spending as little money as possible.

David's probably not the best person to have around during the prenuptial phase: he's so guilty about his continuing relationship with Jessica that he's having visions of her turning up at his house and cooking the rabbit. Pete's furious that David hasn't called the affair off. And, without their advice, Adam ends up buying the most disgusting (and most expensive) engagement ring in the jeweller's shop, an elaborate red rocky affair that looks like it came out of a Christmas cracker. Pleased as punch, he takes it home and presents it to Rachel, and he interprets her speechlessness as an excess of pleasure.

Things aren't going too well for Karen. She doesn't know – yet – that her husband is having an affair, but she's feeling bored, frustrated and neglected. She's started drinking during the day, and is losing patience with all her mumsy friends. Fuelled up on lager, she tells them that other people's babies are boring – apart from one particular baby, who is both boring and ugly. The cracks are beginning to show, and Karen's on a steep downward spiral. There's some distraction from her friends' problems: Rachel has an engagement ring that she hates, and Jenny is on the verge of splitting up with Robert, who's fed up with all her friends ignoring him. Karen has nothing to reproach herself with: of all of them, she's the only one who's made an attempt to be nice to Robert.

The wedding plans are getting out of control. Rachel's found a venue: a monstrously expensive stately home that's had a late cancellation. Adam's horrified, but he realises that this is Rachel's big day and he goes along with it. But then there's the business of the food, the drink, the dresses, the music... As the plans become ever more elaborate, Adam begins to wonder what getting married is really all about.

David, true to his word, decides to finish his affair with Jessica. He takes her to a nice restaurant, and prepares to dump her in the most civilised way possible. But his plans go awry when Robert walks in, also with another woman. They've caught each other out, and David handles it badly. First of all he tells Jessica to hide in the toilets, then he tells Robert that she's 'just a colleague' and that he'll see her back at the office. Jessica, understandably upset by this ungallant behaviour, storms out of the restaurant.

The end of the affair.

On a downward spiral... Karen is arrested.

'You can be an insensitive, patronising, cowardly little prick. Goodbye.'

Jessica's had enough of David

Karen's behaviour is becoming more and more alarming. When she sees a thief trying to break into her car, she gives chase, corners the thief at the car park exit and forces him to run away. She's arrested for her troubles, and calls David from the police station. David is furious: how can she, a married woman, a mother with responsibilities, act so stupidly? Karen's response is cool; she turns to David and asks 'Why did you marry me?'

Jenny's decided to call it a day with Robert. It's not been an easy decision, because little Adam was getting very fond of her new boyfriend, but she realises that Robert just isn't prepared to take her on. Single again, she starts to think about Pete. They got on well in Ireland; the old spark is still there, and Adam needs his dad. Pete comes round to collect Adam, and there's a moment of warm-hearted banter that leads Jenny to imagine she's got a chance of getting her man back. But it's too late. Pete's come to ask her for a divorce.

Rachel is burying her anxieties about the wedding in a frenzy of shopping. She gets Jenny and Karen to try on bridesmaids' dresses ('I look like a toilet dolly', complains Jenny), then, to her horror, loses her engagement ring. She decides not to tell Adam, and goes to the jeweller's to get a new one. It's then that she realises that, far from being a bit of cheap tat, it cost Adam the equivalent of two months' salary. Rachel swallows hard, and buys a replica.

But, in fact, the ring was never lost. Rachel had left it on the toilet cistern, and when Adam confronts her with her carelessness she reveals that she hated the ring all along. Both rings are returned to the shop – prompting Adam and Rachel to realise that the big, splashy, expensive wedding they've been planning is not what they really want. They cancel the stately home and opt instead for a simpler service that will focus on what their marriage really means. David, touched by their predicament, offers to host the wedding reception at his house.

Poor David: he's trying hard to patch things up with Karen, but she's having none of it. A nice meal in a restaurant isn't enough to win her round, and she begins to suspect that there's more to David's sudden charm offensive than meets the eye. Does she suspect the truth? David's walking on eggshells.

Pete and Jenny can't make up their minds about the divorce. Both agree that it's time to move on, but they can't forget how good they were together. For a moment, it looks as if they might make a go of things... but Pete's got a date with Emma, and walks away from Jenny. She's left alone – and he's left wondering whether he's made the right decision.

Episode 8

The wedding day is here and Rachel's mind is on other things... Everyone knows about David except Karen, but not for long... Pete and Jenny decide to give it another go...

The big day is approaching – the day to which all three series of Cold Feet have led, through ups and downs – the wedding of Rachel Bradley and Adam Williams. There were times when it looked as if it would never happen, but now, finally, the guests are gathering to celebrate an enduring love. Pete's contribution, as well as being best man, is to produce the wedding video – and the final stages of preparation are caught on film for posterity.

The day begins with a bachelor breakfast at Adam's house, with the groom and the best man tucking into plates full of sausages that may or may not be poisonous. Naturally, their thoughts turn to marriage, a subject that's close to Pete's heart as he is currently seeking a divorce from Jenny. Adam asks him if he'll ever remarry – but Pete's far from sure that a divorce is what he really wants. He can't help thinking about how great his relationship with Jenny used to be, and now that he sees Adam and Rachel finally settling down he wonders if he's doing the right thing.

Rachel's getting ready at Karen's house. This should really be her big day, but Karen's got other things on her mind. She's begun to suspect that David is having an affair, but so far she has no proof. That proof won't be long in coming. During a bitter scene between Jenny and Robert, during which he gives back the house keys and takes away his few possessions, he reveals that he ran into David in a restaurant with Jessica. Jenny is stunned – but when she turns up at the Marsdens' house, the look on David's face confirms her worst suspicions. With typical bloody-mindedness, Jenny decides that the secret is hers to share, and so as soon as she

Confetti

✿ The large, beautiful and extremely expensive stately home where Rachel wanted to hold the wedding was Tatton Park, near Knutsford in Cheshire. It's a popular marriage venue – and also a popular film location.

'Williams Rachel You
I Love'

Adam's wedding speech

finds Rachel at the registry office she tells her what Karen had only suspected. And now the question remains: should they tell Karen? Well, Rachel reminds Jenny, Karen told you when Pete was having an affair. Somehow the focus seems to have been taken off Rachel on her wedding day, and she becomes obsessed by the idea of setting Karen and David's marriage to rights.

There's a snag back at the groom's house. Firstly, Pete's the only member of the groom's party to be wearing morning dress. Secondly, and more importantly, he's forgotten to organise transport to the registry office. Taxis are in short supply, and in the end there's only one option: trusty David and his Harley. Adam arrives at the town hall in style, leaving Pete, in top hat and tails, to hitch a lift with some nuns.

The wedding party has made it as far as the registry office, but they're still a long way from getting married. Rachel's mind seems to be anywhere except on Adam. She's fighting with her parents; her father's turned up, keen to be the one to give her away, but she's having none of it. She hates her father because, she

Pete hitches a lift.

says, he used to hit her mother, and would rather be given away by David. But then, of course, David is an adulterer, another subject which is preoccupying the bride to be. As David leads her up the aisle, Rachel actually asks him whether it's true that he's been having an affair. When he confesses, Rachel drags him out of the wedding chamber for an emergency conference. The groom, bemused by his bride's behaviour, has a sudden need to go to the toilet.

The registrar is getting impatient, but finally both parties stand before him at the same time, and to everyone's astonishment the best man turns up with his

A rare picture of Rachel with her parents.

video camera. The wedding goes ahead, and finally Adam and Rachel are man and wife.

Back at the reception, all the talk is of David's affair. Karen, of course, is the last to know; everyone else has been up in the toilet discussing the details of her

After a few false starts, the knot is finally tied.

personal life while she's playing hostess downstairs. David, realising that the game's up, decides that Karen had better hear the truth from him. He takes her aside just as Pete is starting his speech, which is interrupted by a loud shriek of 'Shit!' from an adjacent room.

Karen reacts to David's confession with cold fury. He offers to leave, but she commands him to stay. She will not be made a fool of, they will keep up appearances for the sake of the children, but he will sleep in the spare room. As far as Karen is concerned, the marriage is over.

Pete's speech isn't going too well, but then anecdotes about the bride's masturbation habits and former marriages probably aren't the ideal material for a family wedding. Rachel's parents are indignant; they knew nothing of her first marriage, or her divorce. But she's got news for them: her first husband was black, she aborted his baby, she's infertile... and by the way, their other daughter is a lesbian and is living in Australia because she can't stand her parents. Rachel's parents leave abruptly, while a nervous Rachel puts through a call to Sydney.

After the wedding, the gang gathers in Jenny's lounge to watch the wedding video, 'a Pete Gifford film'. It's a mess: not only are crucial scenes missing, but it appears to be spliced with scenes from one of Matthew's porn tapes. Pete doesn't care: he's finished with Emma and he's back with Jenny. At last something's going right for him.

It looks like David and Karen's marriage could be over.

But Pete and Jenny are ready to
try again.

SCENE 62   INT DAVID AND KARENS LOUNGE
TIME   20.35 Night 2

WE JOIN PETE MID-SPEECH. LAUGHTER GREETS SOMETHING HE'S
JUST SAID. PETE CONTINUES...

PETE: Now Adam thinks he knows all there is to know about
Rachel. And let's be honest, eh, there's a great deal to
know. I wasn't going to mention any of it, but this morning
my mate Adam said to me that I can say anything I like.
And do you know what, I'm delighted.

RACHEL LOOKS HORRIFIED AT ADAM.

RACHEL: (WHISPERS, TO ADAM) You said what?!

ADAM: (WHISPERS, TO RACHEL) Don't worry. He promised to be
discreet.

PETE: (TO GUESTS) Now for example, Adam was worried he
might not be man enough for Rachel.

ADAM: (TO RACHEL, SOTTO VOCE) Oh my God. Not the missing
bollock!

PETE: I'm not referring of course to just the one testicle
he has remaining (ADAM RECOILS: "DOH!") but his apparent
inability to satisfy her sexually ladies and gentlemen. Oh
yes. You see, the other week Adam caught Rachel upstairs -
how shall I put this - on the bed "amusing herself". I
think - you know what I mean? (ADAM AND RACHEL BOTH LOOK
MORTIFIED. JENNY IS EMBARRASED) (TO ADAM) Well Adam,
you'll be relieved to know, mate, that the reason that
Rachel was writhing on the bed with her hands fiddling down
their at her crotch, was her jeans were too tight and she
couldn't get the zip up. So that's what it was all about.
(BEAT) But my sources do tell me that she's still not afraid
to play with the one she loves now and again. Regularly.

THE WEDDING GUESTS AREN'T SURE HOW TO TAKE THIS ANECDOTE.
RACHEL'S MUM LEANS IN TO HER DAD.

RACHEL'S MUM: (ASIDE TO HER HUSBAND) What on earth is he on
about?

ADAM, ROLLING HIS EYES, LEANS IN TO RACHEL, WHO'S LOOKING
HORRIFIED BY THESE REVELATIONS.

ADAM: I knew I should have asked David to be my Best Man.

PETE IS AWARE THAT HIS SPEECH IS THUS FAR NOT A RESOUNDING
SUCCESS. HE SMILES ENCOURAGINGLY AT HIS AUDIENCE.

SCENE 64   INT DAVID AND KARENS LOUNGE
TIME   20.45 Night 2

PETE IS STILL ON HIS FEET, DELIVERING HIS SPEECH. THIS (AND
THE AUDIENCE REACTION) IS STILL BEING VIDEOED BY THE GUY
WHO TOOK THE CAMERA FROM HIM.

PETE: (REFERRING TO HIS NOTES) So, yes, Adam Williams finally
gets married. Well, there's a first time for everything isn't
there.   (LOOKS UP, EXTEMPORISES) Not for Rachel. Second
time for her. Bet you didn't know that did you?

A NUMBER OF PEOPLE (INCLUDING RACHEL'S PARENTS) FROWN, NOT
UNDERSTANDING THIS REFERENCE.

RACHEL: (ASIDE) Oh, shit.

PICKING UP ON HIS AUDIENCE'S CONFUSION, PETE FEELS THE NEED
TO EXPLAIN. UNFORTUNATELY IN TRYING TO DIG HIMSELF OUT OF A
HOLE, HE DIGS HIMSELF INTO AN EVEN DEEPER ONE.

PETE: (SEEKING TO REASSURE AUDIENCE) Not that it lasted
long though. Well, it did actually. It lasted ages. Not
until the divorce - that was when Adam found out they were
married. And that when they were just moving in together.
Yeah. And then he moved in as well you know, husband
number one, he moved in .. there was three of them - three
of them together.

RACHEL: (TO HERSELF) Oh shit.

THE MAJORITY OF GUESTS ARE STILL QUITE PERPLEXED (HER
PARENTS LOOKING WELL LESS THAN AMUSED). PETE TRIES TO
RESCUE THE SITUATION WITH CHEERY BONHOMIE.

PETE: It was just like a French film. Still, you have to
laugh, don't you?

PETE LOOKS HAPPILY AT THE AUDIENCE, WHO STARE BACK AT HIM
BLANKLY.

PETE: (CONFIDENCE EBBING) Apparently not.

PETE NERVOUSLY CLEARS HIS THROAT AND FLICKS THROUGH HIS
CARDS, LOOKING FOR A MORE APPROPRIATE TOPIC.

David's Other Women

Natalie (Lorelie King)
She's the all-American ballbreaker, a gutsy and opinionated businesswoman who runs rings around her colleagues and seems to have a special mission to terrorise David. At first, Natalie's a monster; her behaviour at the black-tie charity event, goading Jenny and then demanding an apology for her ruined dress, makes her one of *Cold Feet*'s greatest villains. But later on she emerges in a more sympathetic light. She gets the sack, goes into business on her own and actually gives David a job when he needs it most. Later on she becomes a friend of the family, conspiring with Karen to help celebrate her anniversary to David. Like all the characters in *Cold Feet*, she mellows, and improves, with age.

'I love guys who can't get it up. You tip big. And don't leave a mess.'
Trixie

Trixie (Eva Pope)
David decides that the only way to get over his impotence is to visit "a professional" - and picks Trixie. Like many of her professional clients, David is all talk and no action, but Trixie is an expert in this area as well. She advises him to concentrate on work: regain your manhood there, and you'll soon be a king in the bedroom. And of course she's right.

Jessica (Yasmine Bannerman)

She arrives on the Marsdens' doorstep looking for support for the local residents' association – and ends up wrecking their marriage. It's not really Jessica's fault: she's a nice enough woman, she's on her own, and she finds David very attractive. They make a good team, fighting off the developers in order to save a local playground – but when she lets David know that she's sexually available she throws him into a panic. Arguably she's at fault in starting an affair with a man whom she knows to be married, but David seems like a man that can take care of himself. When he starts lying to her, and pretending that she's just a colleague, Jessica understandably gets the hump and leaves him. David's well aware that he's made a huge mistake, and hopes Karen can forgive him, but it's too late for that.

Robyn Duff (Lucy Robinson)

Right up until the end of his marriage, David believed that there would only ever be one woman for him: Karen. So it's doubly ironic that the final reason why their relationship doesn't work out is because David has fallen for another woman – his divorce lawyer. Robyn is much more David's equal than Karen, more confident, more understanding of his needs and ambitions. At first she's reluctant to get involved, and is furious when David starts to backtrack on their relationship. But outside their professional engagement, they find that they have a lot in common – and Robyn even gets on with David's children. And so, to everyone's surprise – including David's – he ends up with the girl.

Karen Marsden

(HERMIONE NORRIS)

Of all the *Cold Feet* crew, Karen goes on the biggest personal journey of all. She starts out as rather a minor character, a frustrated posh girl who wants it all and gets annoyed when she can't have it. It's hard to feel much sympathy for a woman who has so much but just wants more, more, more – but, as the show progresses, we begin to find out a great deal about Karen Marsden. To know her is not necessarily to love her, but it is certainly to understand her.

There are two great opposing forces in Karen's life, which she will never reconcile. Firstly, there is her social instinct to be a respectable wife, mother and professional, to live a comfortable life in comfortable surroundings, and to enjoy all the benefits that money can bestow. Opposed to that is her appetite for the wild side. In her student days, Karen was a bad girl – well, as bad as any nice middle-class university-going girl can be. She was a member of the Socialist Workers' Party, she went on marches, she drank and took drugs and had a lot of sex with a lot of different people. She and Rachel had some high times together – and it was always Karen who would push things just a little bit further. She had a taste for extremes even then, but she tried to bury it when she met David. David rescued Karen – not just from the man who was giving her grief at a party (David flattened him) but from a life she wasn't sure she wanted. If David hadn't come along, Karen might have done anything: she could have ended up getting into a lot of scrapes, but she might equally have found happiness in a much more unconventional lifestyle. As it is she opted for the kind of life that she was brought up to expect, marrying an eminently suitable man, settling down in a nice suburb of Manchester and proceeding to raise children.

At first, her only dissatisfaction is over the fact that she doesn't have a nanny. But as time goes by, the old Karen starts to surface more and more. She gets fed up with her friends, all those boring business associates of David's who can only talk about nannies and skiing and house prices. She tires quickly of the endless round of the school run, of talking to other mothers about their precious little babies as if that's all that matters in life. She longs for excitement and adventure – and David, for all his virtues, is not the man for that. And so Karen starts, slowly but surely, to go off the rails. It starts harmlessly: a flirtation

> **'You have dope on your bedside table, I have the latest Joanna Trollope.'**
>
> Karen bemoans her life

The epitome of the affluent middle-class couple... and that was half the problem for Karen.

with one of her authors which comes to nothing, but is enough to send Karen scuttling back to the security of married life. And then she starts taking the odd joint after dinner, making rude jokes, getting tattoos. David doesn't understand where this behaviour is coming from: it's obvious that there's a whole side of Karen's life that she's kept well and truly hidden. It's the side that she sacrificed for

Karen is a modern woman trapped by circumstances. In the first series she had a young child, then she had twins — and she's never been able to fulfil her potential because she wanted to stay at home with the children. As a result everyone labels her as a mother and doesn't take much notice of her opinions. It was hard, as a writer, to find much for her to do, because she didn't get out of the house too often. But gradually, Karen broke out of that domestic prison. My favourite moment was when she smoked a joint at a dinner party and shocked all her boring friends: she started to rebel, and that's when she got interesting. But she could never really walk away from her respectable middle-class life, however much she wanted to. She's kicking against a situation that, ultimately, she created for herself, and that makes her quite hard. Jenny often appears to be the hardest of the **Cold Feet** women, but Karen is the hard one.

respectability, and it won't stay suppressed for long.

Of course, Karen meets her nemesis at the bottom of a bottle. Her rapid descent into alcoholism surprises nobody more than Karen — but what starts out as regular drinking has soon become a full-blown sickness. She has to sink pretty low before she realises just what's going on — but once she finds herself shoeless in a muddy carpark fighting off the attentions of a slobbering drunk, she realises that things have gone too far. Luckily for Karen, she's not that far gone that she can't find the road back, and all it takes is a couple of trips to the therapist and a bit of will-power and she kicks alcohol for good.

It might seem that Karen has escaped her demons, but more damage has been done than she realises. There's only so many times a man can be rejected before he seeks comfort elsewhere and Karen's dissatisfaction has driven David into the arms of another woman. When he realises what he's doing, David runs back to Karen and seeks forgiveness — but Karen's dignity is forever wounded. Her refusal to understand the motives for David's infidelity say a great deal about Karen, and the way in which she blames others for her own problems. And of

Karen and Mark, the affair didn't last, but the damage to her marriage was irreparable.

course, when she is tempted by Mark, she suddenly realises that adultery is only a hotel room away.

Karen emerges from her relationship with Mark a very different woman. She's realised that the most important things in her life are her children – but by that time it's too late to rebuild a relationship with their father. She's pushed David away so effectively that he won't come back to have his nose rubbed in the dirt again. At the end of the final series, Karen is alone . It's possible, of course, that David will come back to her – marriages in *Cold Feet* tend to be made of India rubber, and can bounce back and forward for ever – but nobody, least of all Karen, would put money on it.

Loves

♡ Adventure

♡ Booze

♡ Her job

♡ David and Mark

Hates

⑥ Respectability

⑥ Daily drudgery

⑥ Boredom

⑥ David and Mark

Hermione Norris

(Karen Marsden)

Hermione Norris has taken the character of Karen Marsden from two-dimensional beginnings to a fully-rounded finale over the course of five series of *Cold Feet*. 'She was a bit of a stereotype in the pilot,' says Norris. 'I played her as very posh, very much a twinset and pearls type of girl. To be honest, I hated myself in the pilot, and when we came to make the series I changed the characterisation completely. I even changed the voice. Mike started to write the character differently, and made her more sympathetic, even though it took time for her storylines to take off. But the biggest difference, if you look back, is between the pilot and the first series.'

Karen's trajectory has been the most dramatic of the six main *Cold Feet* characters. She starts off as a conservative, wealthy woman trapped in a dull, conventional marriage, and goes through a series of life-changing experiences which leave her, if not happy, at least liberated. 'In the first couple of series, Karen was trapped in a world of downtrodden domesticity. The whole dynamic between Karen and David was well established: he'd wind her up, she'd feel frustrated, she'd make barbed, witty little comments as a way of getting her own back. She was wry and funny but she was actually quite oppressed. She was always watching what other people did, commenting on it but not really being part of it. Then at the end of series three she started having an affair, and I can't tell you what a relief that was. It's very hard to play someone who is continually internalising experience, whose only role is to observe and comment and to make little bitchy asides. It was nice to open the door on Karen and explore some of her interior world. Everything that was covert became overt. She'd had her moments before: she nearly had an affair with one of her writers, and she'd started smoking dope at dinner parties. But it was really when she started drinking and having an affair that she became interesting. She actually started living a life of her own, even though she was making some terrible judgements. I can't say I approved of what she did, but as an actress I was very glad. It was just such a relief to have some stimulating material to work with, and I attacked it with relish. It's always much more fun to be bad than good.'

For Hermione, the secret of *Cold Feet*'s success lies in the characterisations. 'All the main characters are based on people in Mike Bullen's life,' she says. 'We actually met them in the early days, and I'm astonished that they're all still friends, especially the people on whom he based Karen and David. They were such unsympathetic characters in the early series! But after we'd been going for a couple of years, the characters took on a life of their own, and they became much more real. Audiences started to relate to them a lot more. Whatever situation the characters were put into - and some of them were pretty far-fetched - they always seemed real because the characters were real. I think people appreciated that. I mean, we're not a particularly attractive bunch. We're not the beautiful people. We're just normal people going through normal things in life, we're vulnerable and very fallible. I think that's a relief for audiences, because they see that life's like that, that other people are going through bad experiences just like they are. And over time you learned to understand the characters, and once you understand someone you generally like them.

'I know that a lot of people felt that Karen was very hard on David after he'd had his affair, but I had a lot of women telling me that they could understand exactly what she was doing. Karen worked herself into a position where there was no more room to manoeuvre; her pride got the better of her, and she couldn't move on. It's not a particularly admirable quality, but it's something we've all done. I'm full of admiration for Mike Bullen, because he took these six people and wrote that amount of material about them, he made their lives weave in and out in that way, and he never once lost sight of who they were. In fact, they all grew and became more realistic.'

The final series sees resolution of a kind for Karen: her marriage to David is irretrievably over, and she faces an uncertain future as a single parent. 'It's a long, long way from where she started. The old Karen could never have believed that she'd end up on her own. But she made certain choices and had certain experiences that led her, step by step, to this situation that isn't fully in her control. I wish, actually, that the whole experience of her divorce had been explored more fully in the fifth series: we could have gone a lot deeper into her character then, as she tried to choose between David and Mark. In the event, I think it was rather thrown away. But I can see why: the whole series was leading up to one main event, the death of Rachel, and everything else was sacrificed to that.'

The success of Cold Feet caught Norris, like many of the cast, unawares. 'When you're involved in a show, you just get on with it, you do your job and you go home at the end of the day. You don't suddenly sit up and go 'Oh my God! I'm in a fantastic hit!'. Of course there are awards and press and things, but the reality of making a show like Cold Feet is you spend your life sitting in a car park in the north of England wondering how the hell you're going to learn your lines, when you're going to get home. I'm sure I'll look back on it in the future and realise that it was the most amazing job, but at the moment it's hard to have that kind of perspective. Actors are very different from the characters they play.

At the end, Karen is left alone, a single mother with three children.

They go home at the end of the day and their lives carry on as normal. We're not going on those big emotional journeys, and the job doesn't leave that kind of mark. You don't really change; it's people's perception of you that changes.'

Happily for Hermione, the profession now perceives her as a highly employable actress. Between the fourth and fifth series, she worked 11 months out of 12, usually doing six-day weeks. 'I flew straight back from Australia and went to Newcastle to start work on the first series of *Wire in the Blood*, with Robson Green. Then I went to London to shoot a docudrama about domestic violence called *Falling Apart*. I had a few weeks off, then started *Cold Feet* again. I can't carry on working like that; I'd like to have my own life back, please.'

As a move in the right direction, Norris celebrated the end of *Cold Feet* by marrying her partner; at the time of writing she's attached to 'various projects which are waiting for a green light.' It's unlikely that she'll be short of work. 'I know people's memories are short, so it's important for me to capitalise on the success of *Cold Feet*; it's something we're all very conscious of. Once the show's been off the screen for a couple of years, people will forget about us. So I need to do a good variety of work now while I've got the opportunity. I've had to turn so much down in the last few years, because of *Cold Feet* - being in a successful show like that is a mixed blessing. It raises your profile, but it makes it very hard to take on jobs. If I'd known when I signed up that *Cold Feet* was going to take up such a huge chunk of my life, I would maybe have had second thoughts. Of course I'm immensely grateful to the show, because it's the best job I've done, and the biggest thing I expect I'll ever do, but the time is definitely right to move on.'

Jo

(KIMBERLEY JOSEPH)

Jo likes a drink, a laugh and a late night. She seems like the typical young Australian woman – open minded, free spirited, without a care in the world, and as such she's attractive company for all the Cold Feet gang. Rachel and Karen immediately cleave to her as a kindred spirit: Jo represents a kind of guilt-free hedonism towards which both aspire. But we soon discover that there's more to Jo than

'My dad thinks you're a piece of shit... he may be right.'

Jo is not happy with Pete

meets the eye. She has low self-esteem, which she hides behind the mask of the up-for-it ladette. She uses sex as a way of boosting her confidence, because she knows that she can get blokes without too much difficulty. Holding on to them, however, is a different matter. Most of the men she gets involved with just think of Jo as a good-time

girl, not as a serious proposition for a relationship. The depths of Jo's disillusionment comes when she starts dating her boss, and discovers that he's passed her over for a promotion rather than risking office gossip about them being lovers.

Loves
♡ Partying
♡ Sex
♡ Laughing
♡ Pete's humour

Hates
☺ Lack of commitment
☺ Her boss
☺ Herself
☺ Not getting her way

A lot of Jo's problems stem from her experiences in Australia. The beloved daughter of a wealthy father, she's used to getting her way – but her long-term relationship with fiancé Shawn fell to pieces when he seemed to be shying away from marriage. Rather than working things out and confronting their problems, Jo fled to London where she tried to reinvent her life. But she soon finds the old problems resurfacing when she starts going out with Suggs, a student from her aerobics class. He likes her, she's a laugh, they have a good sex life – but beyond that they have nothing in common. In fact, the only man she seems to have anything in common with is her landlord, Pete. But Pete is... well... Pete. It takes Jo some time to realise that not only is Pete the nicest

man she's ever met, but he's also head over heels in love with her.

Their courtship is brief and intense. Convinced that she's not interested in him, Pete gives her the cold shoulder, and Jo, true to form, runs back to Australia. But Pete follows her, she proposes marriage and they overcome paternal resistance and live happily ever after. Until series five, that is, when Pete's self-destructive urges smash the marriage to pieces. Jo can't convince him that she married him for love, rather than for a visa, and when Pete's hostility drives her into the arms of Lee, Jo realises that there's no real trust or love between her and her husband. And for Jo, the only solution to that problem is to escape. This time she goes back to Australia for good.

Kimberley Joseph

(Jo)

Kimberley Joseph was in Los Angeles, struggling to break into American films and TV, when her agent called her with an audition for a British show called *Cold Feet*. 'To be honest, I'd never heard of it, and neither had my agent, but I went along to the audition to give it a go,' says Joseph. 'I met Spencer Campbell, the producer, and we chatted about life and the world for about half an hour, then I did my bit, and that was that. At the time, I just wanted to get out of LA. I was struggling a bit, and I wanted to go home to Australia, where I had an appointment to sort out my green card so I could come back and try again. But I was really ready to leave. So I guess I went into the audition with a don't-care attitude; I thought the game was up in LA and I wanted to get out. And obviously that was the right attitude! As soon as you stop wanting something, you get it. I've found that to be a rule in my life.'

Kimberley didn't hear anything for a couple of weeks, and travelled to the desert for a short break before returning home. 'When I finally got to a place where I could get a signal on my phone, there were about ten messages from Spencer asking me to get in touch. I cancelled my trip to Australia, and within three days I was in Manchester for the first readthrough. I still didn't know anything about the show; they only got videos to me after the readthrough, and I watched them in my hotel room and started to realise that this was something really big. Actually, it wasn't a bad way of doing it. If I'd known what I was coming into, I would have been really nervous. I had no idea of how successful the show was until we were walking around the streets in Manchester and people were calling out the characters' names.'

The character of Jo was introduced slowly. At first she was nothing more than a colleague of Rachel's, an easy-going Australian girl who liked a drink and a good time. 'I knew all along that she'd been brought in as Pete's new love interest,' says Kimberley, 'but it was important that she was established in her own right first. I think there would have been a lot of hostility towards her if she'd come straight in as Pete's girlfriend. Jenny was such an important part of the show that people still had a sense of loyalty to her. They had to get to know and like Jo for herself before she became involved with Pete.'

Jo proved to be a tonic for the show as well as for Pete. 'It was the right time to bring in some new blood. Jo's a free spirit, she's got that typical Aussie directness, she shoots from the hip. It was good for the show to have someone who could say what she thought, without worrying about the consequences. Australians aren't known for being terribly PC; we're pretty unedited. So Jo could say 'For God's sake, David, snap out of it!', which none of the others would do. I

New girl on the block. Kimberley provided a breath of fresh air for *Cold Feet*.

think Mike Bullen had something much coarser in mind at first, a kind of big fat truck-driving lesbian type, but I don't think I'm quite that.'

Kimberley was already well known in Australia, where *Cold Feet* is shown to a large and enthusiastic audience. She'd starred in *Home and Away* ((as Joanne Brennan) and presented *Australian Gladiators* for a few years. 'I was doing well at home, but I wanted to get away from that soap-star/TV presenter image and do some proper acting. That's why I went to LA. But there is so much competition there. I know it's a cliché, but it's a really hard town to succeed in. I'd done a short TV series at home called *Tales of the South Seas*, which I hoped would be my entrée to the States, but it didn't get picked up and I was stuck in LA with no work. That's not easy. Everyone's so focused on getting a job, and if you're not working you're nobody. After that it was a relief to come to Manchester, which is a real city with real people, where you don't have to have a car, you can walk around the streets and live a normal life.'

No sooner was Kimberley part of the cast than the producers announced that the show was on its travels – to Australia. 'So I had my big homecoming after all. It was a great way for me to shed that soap image; I was coming home in a big successful show, and I'd be taken more seriously. Going to Sydney with the *Cold Feet* crew was amazing. I lived there for four years, so I could take them to all my favourite bars and beaches. And I'm very proud that it was the Australian episode of *Cold Feet* that won the Bafta.'

Now that *Cold Feet* is over, and Jo's returned to Australia, Kimberley's back on the job market with a greatly enhanced CV. 'I'll be going back to LA to try my luck there again. *Cold Feet* will help, but only a bit; I'm not kidding myself that this is my big break in Hollywood, because Hollywood is full of actors who have been in TV shows all over the world. I'd like to do more work in the UK as well, but the real opportunities are in the States. I guess I'll be all over the place in the next few years – the US, the UK, Australia. It's okay, but it's an unsettled life. I hope one day there will be a man who'll pin me down to just one place.'

Series 4

18 Nov - 10 Dec 2001 ⑤ 8 episodes

The **spotlight** shifts to the Marsdens' troubled marriage. David's affair with Jessica is over, and he's truly repentant - but that's not enough for Karen, who's determined to punish him, and herself, and the children if it comes to that. She starts **drinking** heavily, Ramona leaves her employment and David goes to sleep in Pete's spare room. Eventually, realising that she's making a complete hash of her life, Karen pours all her booze down the sink and allows David to come home. But just when it looks as if things are getting back on to an even keel, she meets Mark. And suddenly **adultery** doesn't seem like such a very bad idea after all...

Pete's getting used to being **single again**. Jenny's decided to start a new life in New York, taking Adam Junior with her - and suddenly Pete discovers that he can pull women. But he's not the **promiscuous** type; what he's looking for is a full-time relationship. But it seems that nobody can replace Jenny... until he meets Jo. **Friendship** turns to love, and Pete pursues her to Australia for a whirlwind courtship and marriage.

Adam and Rachel are the most settled of all the couples, despite the **occasional hiccup** (particularly in the shape of Adam's old flame-turned-stalker Jane Fitzpatrick). Now they're thinking of starting a family, and it seems that the only way to go about it is to adopt. Until, that is, Rachel falls pregnant...

Series 4

Episode 1

Is Rachel having an affair?... Jenny and Pete have settled back into married life... David's taken to reading poetry... Karen's taken to drinking

After a long and unsatisfactory career as Manchester's most unemployable temp, Jenny is finally finding some kind of job satisfaction as a secretary for Claiborne Hotels, a trendy, rapidly-expanding chain. But at the start of the show her mind isn't exactly on her work: she thinks she may be pregnant, and once again goes through the anxieties of taking a test. It proves positive – which means that she and Pete are about to be parents again. For Jenny, this is life-changing news: she's prepared to put her career on hold, to settle her differences with Pete and make a fresh start as a family. For once, the future looks good for the Giffords.

Rachel has a new hobby. But Adam's not too happy about it.

Rachel, meanwhile, seems to be playing away from home. We see her in a passionate clinch with a man who is most definitely not Adam. Have things gone wrong so soon after their wedding? No – in fact, Rachel is discovering an interest in amateur dramatics, and has signed up for a fringe production that involves a good deal of sex. It's something she's always wanted to do, but, given the nature of the show, she's not over-eager to share the news with Adam or the rest of the gang. So of course it's only a matter of time before everyone knows what Rachel's up to behind Adam's back – and why she's going out in her lunch-hour to buy sexy lingerie. It's her costume.

Adam has a new interest as well: at David's request, he's coaching Josh's under-sevens football team, and begins to fancy himself as a superstar-manager in the making.

Things aren't going too well for David and Karen. They've just celebrated their ninth wedding anniversary, and they're keeping a brave face on things for the sake of the children, but beneath the surface their relationship has gone sour. Karen is determined not to forgive David for his affair with Jessica, and she's rapidly turning into a bitter, resentful woman. David is truly repentant and tries everything he can think of to prove himself to Karen, but she's having none of it. They maintain separate bedrooms; end of story. In desperation, David turns to a local radio phone-in show, the *Love Doctor*, for some advice on his marriage – hoping, perhaps, that Karen will hear him telling the DJ how much he loves her and how much he regrets his past mistakes. But Karen's oblivious to everything; the only person listening in the Marsden household is Ramona, whose sympathies switch entirely to David, and she starts hugging him for no apparent reason. Adam's advice is, for once, sensible: David must turn himself into the man that Karen always wanted him to be – and if this means reading romantic poetry and watching arty foreign films, so be it. So David bravely sits through *The Spirit of the Beehive* (much to Ramona's delight: it's one of her favourite films) and starts boning up on Keats – and Karen seems to be just the tiniest bit impressed.

Jenny's busy at work one day when a handsome stranger enters the office and starts asking her all about Claiborne Hotels. She gives her usual sassy answers – and then discovers, to her horror, that the inquisitive customer is none other than Owen Claiborne, the owner of the chain. She thinks she's about to get the sack again – but instead Owen realises her potential and sends her on a research trip to Rome, to see how Claiborne Hotels are really run. Jenny's delighted: a free trip, a chance to prove her mettle, and a couple of days off from being a mum. She leaves Adam Junior with his godfather, and takes Pete as her guest. Pete, of course, is delighted: surely a romantic few days in the Eternal City with his pregnant wife means that the marriage is well and truly back on course.

Things don't go quite as Pete would like; Jenny's very much in work mode, and hangs around the hotel proving to all and sundry what a wonderful manager she could be. Pete's left to wander the city on his own – but he's stoical about the experience, hoping that it's a precursor of better times to come.

Back home, Adam and Rachel seem to have hit a sticky patch. He does not approve of her theatrical endeavours: he turned up uninvited to a rehearsal and saw his wife kissing passionately with another man, who was far too attractive for Adam's liking. To make matters worse, Rachel's co-star is suspiciously good looking. Adam throws a big strop and storms out of the rehearsal, dragging a

mortified Rachel with him. A big can of worms has been well and truly opened. Adam doesn't like Rachel's acting; Rachel is fed up of Adam's football coaching. Having Adam Junior to stay isn't helping matters; it just makes them even more tense about the fact that they can't have children. Into this emotional maelstrom steps the director, who was so impressed by Adam's Brandoesque outburst that he offers him a part in the play. Suddenly, the theatre doesn't seem like such a bad idea...

There's a new girl in town: Jo, a colleague of Rachel, a hard-drinking, party-loving Australian who takes great delight in leading Rachel and her friends astray. Soon Jo and Karen are thick as thieves: Jo provides exactly the sort of outlet that Karen needs from the stifling atmosphere back home, and together they start exploring Manchester's nightlife. Chatted up by two men on the dance floor, they go their separate ways: Karen back home to face a hangover and a Keats-quoting husband, Jo back for a night of sexual athletics with her new conquest. Karen realises that she doesn't really want to be young, free and single... and perhaps, after all, David is making a real effort.

The day of the big match arrives, and Adam is confident that the Didsbury Devils have a good chance of getting through the first round of the Manchester Under-Sevens Cup. But things don't seem to work out on the pitch – and, when the team are 12–0 down at half time, Adam gets his marching orders. A great career is nipped in the bud.

Rachel's acting is going a little better; goaded by the director into a more emotional reading of a line about motherhood, Rachel bursts into real tears and reveals to Adam the depth of her distress about her infertility. Forced to realise that the parenting issue is driving a wedge between them, they agree to pursue alternatives – and that means adopting.

Pete and Jenny are back from Rome, in high spirits. For Jenny, it was a personal triumph: Owen has offered her a job as his PA in New York. Pete, of course, is dead against the idea, and Jenny's decided to put her family first and to stay in Manchester to be a full-time mother. And so, their future seemingly secure, Pete and Jenny report to the hospital for an ante-natal scan. But the scan reveals that there is no foetal heartbeat. The baby is dead – and suddenly the future looks very different.

Rachel's show opens, and her friends dutifully turn up to lend their support. Even David is there, in an effort to impress Karen with his new-found culture. But the play is ghastly, the audience leaves in droves, Karen and Jo go off to find a drink – and David is left on his own to face the second half.

In Bed with the *Cold Feet* gang.

Episode 2

Jenny and Pete recover from their loss... Rachel and Adam decide to adopt... Will David and Karen ever sort out their differences... Adam bumps into an old friend.

Jenny is sick of getting bunches of flowers from all her friends. They want to show their support in the wake of her miscarriage, but it's an inappropriately funereal gesture – and Jenny responds in her usual way, by losing her temper and storming out of the room. The situation's not helped by tactless Rachel, who announces that she and Adam have decided to adopt a child. Shamed by their lack of sensitivity, the gang bin the flowers and buy Jenny a jumbo-sized box of chocolates, a far more welcome gift all round.

Things are going from bad to worse chez Marsden. Karen is drinking heavily, picking fights with David over the smallest things – and it hasn't escaped Josh's notice. Pained by his parents' constant rows, he turns to Ramona, who doesn't know how to explain the complexities of a marital breakdown to a small child. For the first time, Ramona thinks seriously about leaving Karen and David – especially as she's not short of tempting offers from elsewhere. A club owner has spotted her talents at her salsa class, and offered her a job as a table dancer in one of his venues. And the Marsdens' neighbours, Georgina and Lewis, are keen to poach her to look after their own children.

Adam and Rachel take their first steps on the long, rocky road to adoption. A preliminary meeting at the agency doesn't go well; Adam's at odds with the prevailing views on parenthood, and makes a major faux-pas by admitting that he would, if pushed, smack a child. This is the wrong answer; many of the kids up for adoption come from abusive backgrounds. It seems that Adam's fallen at the first hurdle. But the social worker is convinced that he's willing to learn, and gives them another chance. Adam's mind isn't entirely on the matter in hand; he's run into Jane Fitzpatrick in Manchester, and to his horror she's making friends with Rachel and getting herself invited round for dinner. Will the embarrassing truth about his stag night finally emerge?

Karen is falling apart. Babysitting for Jenny and Pete one night, she has to leave little Adam in the care of Jo and run home to look after her own children; she's forgotten that it's Ramona's night off, and for once the babysitter won't take no for an answer. Of course, it's all David's fault; he was meant to be looking after the kids, but instead he was out seeing a therapist, trying to make sense of his

Ramona finds the lure of cash too tempting to resist.

wreck of a marriage. It's another well-meaning gesture that's gone belly-up – and Karen won't listen to any explanations. Jenny comes home to find her son in the care of a woman she's never met before, and is furious. For her, it's the end of a terrible evening. She'd been out for dinner with Pete to tell him that, after all, she's decided to take the job in New York City. He's dead set against the idea, and refuses to come with her. It seems, at last, that they've reached the end of the line. New York isn't the issue: since her miscarriage, Jenny's realised that the rapprochement with Pete will never work out.

The aftershock of this disastrous evening

The sight of his nanny pole dancing proves too much for David.

is quick to follow. Karen takes it out on Ramona, who responds by handing in her notice; she's now working as a table dancer, and has been made an attractive offer by Georgina and Lewis. David begs her to stay, but Karen's adamant: Ramona must leave right now, without even saying goodbye to Josh. And when David runs into Ramona dancing in a club where he's entertaining clients, he too insists that she leave his employment immediately.

Adam's walking on eggshells when Jane comes round for dinner. How much will she tell Rachel about their past? And why is she here in the first place? Finally Jane admits to Adam that her presence in Manchester is not just a coincidence; after their reunion in Ireland she decided to follow him and get him back. For Adam, that spells deep, dark trouble. His marriage is already under a lot of strain thanks to the adoption, and the last thing he needs is a needy ex-girlfriend on the scene.

David's therapy is going well. Guided by his analyst, he realises that his own adultery may be explained by long-buried memories of his father's affair with his mother's sister. Finally he understands what's going on, and he decides to make an all-out attempt to get his marriage back on track. Karen's friends are all telling her to stop being such a martyr, to forgive David and start again – and the final piece of the jigsaw falls into place when David meets a remorseful Ramona in the park with the neighbours' ghastly children, and gives her her job back. Overjoyed, he announces to Karen that the time is right for them to make a new start; Karen responds by telling David to move out of the marital home.

The end of the line for Pete and Jenny...

To polish off an unusually downbeat episode, Jenny prepares to leave for New York. Adam and Rachel host her going-away party, and it's a sombre affair. Pete takes Jenny and Adam Junior to the airport and sees them off into departures – and is left holding his son's fluffy toy rabbit in his hand...

...And Pete is left holding the bunny.

Episode 3 (written by Mike Bullen and Mark Chappell)

Pete gets a new lodger... Adam lets the cat out of the bag
about Jane... Karen sinks to a new low

David and Karen's marriage seems to be in terminal meltdown. He's moved
out of the house and is sleeping in Pete's spare room – a situation that doesn't
suit either of them. Back at home, Karen is drinking more and more heavily. She
plans a girls' night in, at which she knocks back the booze, tells one of her oldest
friends, Bella, that she's become a boring old frump, and then passes out. The
others are so used to Karen's drinking that they hardly notice – and besides,
they're much more interested in talking about sex. Rachel's there, with Jane
Fitzpatrick, who starts to reminisce about her first sexual experience on a bench
in Ireland. She names no names... but the truth is dangerously close to the
surface.

The whole Jane situation is starting to get a little out of hand. Pete's already
warned Adam that he should stop seeing her, that he's playing with fire – which
makes it doubly difficult for Adam when Jane turns up unexpectedly in the
kitchen, where he's cooking a full hangover breakfast for Rachel wearing only an
apron. Jane, who stayed the night after getting drunk round at Karen's, takes

Adam provides the thrills after Jane and Rachel's girly evening.

Out on the town with Pete, Karen gets out of control

advantage of the situation to prove that Adam still finds her attractive. Rachel walks in on a potentially compromising situation – but she doesn't twig. Not yet; for the time being her mind is too focused on adoption to worry about Adam's exes.

Adam, too, is getting tense about the adoption process, and finds himself arguing with Rachel over every minor point. In the past, he'd have taken his troubles straight to Jenny – but she's not around any more. And so, in search of a sympathetic female ear, he finds himself spending more and more time with Jane. During a discussion with Rachel, Adam lets slip that he's been out for a drink with his ex – and at last Rachel starts to get suspicious.

Pete's discovering the joys of the singles scene, and after a successful conquest in the pub with Adam he starts bringing home a different woman every night. He seems to be developing into a full-blown Lothario, much to the amazement of Adam and David, but in a quiet moment Pete admits that it's all a façade, a way of distracting himself from the pain he's feeling after Jenny and Adam's departure.

Karen's out of control. She decides that Pete would be a good drinking partner, and so she drags him off to a bar where she promptly leaves him to his own devices and proceeds to get off with the bar owner, Rick. Pete tags along when they go on to a club, determined to keep Karen out of trouble, but when he tries to persuade her to go home she tells him to get lost. Reluctantly, Pete leaves her with Rick, who takes this as his signal to make a move. Karen is forced to fight him off with her shoe, and he leaves her, drunk, dishevelled and hobbling, in the car park. Even Karen realises that her life is unravelling.

Adam's uncertain what to do about Jane. Should he buy her an old Roxy Music CD and rekindle their romance? Or should he take Pete's advice and just avoid trouble? In the end he achieves a

Clubbing it

Karen and Pete's wild night out took cast and crew on a pub crawl round the city centre. Scenes in clubs and bars in *Cold Feet* are usually filmed out of hours, with extras standing in for the regulars – but on this occasion, for that extra touch of realism, Karen and her pick-up Rick went off to the Music Box in Oxford Road while the club was actually open. Hand-held cameras added to the drunken atmosphere.

'You've no personality left. It's like you've been taken over by aliens.'

Karen loses a friend

compromise: he gives her the CD as a parting present and tells her that she was wrong to follow him to Manchester, that the past is the past and his future is with Rachel. Jane is furious and threatens to tell Rachel everything. A few days later, when Adam comes home to find Jane and Rachel talking together, he immediately assumes the worst and accuses Jane of being a bitch. Nothing really happened, he insists, we just kissed, had a few drinks... But in fact, Jane has come to say goodbye. She realises that Adam was right, she's going back to Ireland to forget about him. But now the cat is out of the bag...

Karen and David put on a public display of unity by attending Josh's school violin recital. It's torture for Karen, who can only think of the drinks that follow the music. On the way home, she loses control of the car and has a minor accident, confessing to David that she'd also had a few drinks before coming out. David manages to fob the police off by telling them he was driving, but, once they're out of the way, he rounds on Karen and tells her exactly what he thinks of her behaviour. She's selfish, she's drunk, she's putting her child's life at risk, to say nothing of ruining his. It's time she pulled herself together.

Karen realises that he's right, and decides to seek professional help. She turns up for her first appointment with the therapist, only to see David coming out of his office. Finally admitting that she's partly to blame for their marriage breakdown, she agrees to stop drinking and to get her life back on track.

Drink driving with her son in the car. Karen hits rock bottom

Episode 4

Rachel exacts her revenge... Pete gets a dog... and another lodger... Karen's on the wagon... Adam and Rachel meet their new daughter.

Rachel is on the warpath. She's furious about Adam and Jane, she's furious with Pete and David for covering up for him, and generally she's acting like a self-righteous pain in the arse. Nothing Adam can do will make her forgive him. He buys her flowers; she chops the heads off. He makes a vase with the word 'sorry' picked out on it; she smashes it into pieces. In a moment of jaw-dropping insensitivity, she starts ranting at David about Adam's infidelity. That's enough for David: he tells her that, in fact, nothing happened between Adam and Jane. She has nothing to forgive – unlike Adam who, Rachel will remember, actually forgave her for sleeping with her ex-boyfriend and all the disastrous aftermath. Rachel, duly chastened, realises that she has some ground to make up, and goes home to bed to await Adam's return – naked but for a Manchester United shirt.

Pete's decided to get himself a dog for company, and so to his already crowded bachelor accommodation is added the messy but affectionate Cantona. David's not overjoyed; the place is a mess as it is. But help is at hand: Audrey, Pete's mother, turns up unexpectedly and immediately starts getting the place into shape. It's certainly nice for the boys to have a cook and cleaner on the premises, but Pete begins to wonder what, exactly, his mother is doing.

Karen, determined to take control of her life, has poured every bottle of wine in the house down the sink. But she's dismayed to learn that Josh's behaviour at school is being affected by the problems at home; he's becoming withdrawn and unpredictable in lessons. David immediately blames the school, and decides the best thing for the boy would be to go to a private school like the one he himself attended as a child. Karen's not so sure, but, given the precarious domestic situation, there's very little that she can say against the idea.

Adam and Rachel are friends again: just as well, as their adoption application is up before the board, and they're about to find out whether or not they'll be approved as prospective parents. After an agony of waiting, they get the green light – and, to their astonishment, they discover that Ruth, the social worker, has a child in mind for them. Eight-year-old Laura is in foster care after being rejected by her heroin-addict mother, and she's ready for a new home. Adam and Rachel can't wait to meet her. The first encounter goes well; Adam and Laura bond by

Adam falls for Laura.

doing Simpsons impersonations, and she's immediately drawn to Rachel as a mother figure. The future seems sunny.

Pete and David return home one day to find the fire brigade in attendance after Audrey had an accident with the chip pan. Shaken by the events, she confesses that it's not the first time things like that have happened; she's getting forgetful, and is scared for her own safety. That's the real reason she came to stay with Pete. Pete's immediate response is to invite her to live with him, although he realises that a divorced man living with his mum isn't exactly an attractive proposition to the opposite sex. But Audrey won't hear of it, and together they start to investigate sheltered accommodation.

They find a suitable place, and Pete, with very mixed feelings, drops his mother off in her new home. He also decides that he'd be better off without Cantona as well, but after handing him over at the dog home he's overwhelmed by guilt and gets him back. He then decides that he should have his mother back as well – but Audrey's quite happy in her new home with her new friends. She even agrees to take on Cantona as well. Pete's a happy man.

David and Karen can't agree over Josh's education, and finally they confront the fact that the school isn't the issue, it's Josh's home life. Tentatively, Karen agrees to David moving back in with her.

Adam and Rachel are busy planning their life as a family, when all of a sudden a bombshell drops.

Rachel is pregnant.

Rachel and Laura bond immediately.

'The truly liberated woman is the woman who does what she wants.'

Episode 5

David's back home... Rachel's pregnant... Pete gets another new lodger...Jo starts whipping the boys into shape...Karen meets a very attractive man.

The news of Rachel's pregnancy spreads like wildfire. Nobody can believe it! Surely Rachel couldn't have children? Isn't that why they're adopting? And, speaking of the adoption, doesn't this change things? Not according to Adam and Rachel: they're still delighted at the prospect of becoming Laura's parents, and are getting used to taking her out for hamburgers. And Laura's up for it as well, especially when she sees 'her' room for the first time and notices that there's a phone point in the wall. That's her idea of heaven... Well, it would be, if they'd paint the room pink.

Pete's just getting used to having the house back to himself, now that David's returned to Karen, when a new guest turns up: Jo. She's walked out of her job, she can't pay her rent and the landlord's kicked her out, so she's forced to throw herself on the mercy of her friends. Adam and Rachel are too busy preparing things for Laura, Karen and David are at a delicate stage in their marriage, and that leaves Pete – who, after all, does have a spare room. And so Jo becomes Pete's lodger, although he gleefully pretends to Adam that he picked her up in a pub the night before.

David's delighted to be back home, and thinks that this marks the beginning of a new chapter in his marriage. Karen's less enthusiastic, but willing to make a go of things for the sake of the children. And then, at a boring party, she meets Mark. She's instantly attracted: Mark is good-looking, intelligent, funny, and works in publishing. More to the point, he's looking for someone to help him edit a women's lifestyle book. A little flattery gets him what he wants, and Karen agrees to have a look at the manuscript.

Pete hosts a barbecue to celebrate Adam and Rachel's news: Rachel is now four months pregnant, and had ascribed her late periods to anxiety over the adoption. Adam begins to suspect that Pete fancies Jo, and does everything he can to make things awkward for the two of them. When Jo announces that she's thinking of setting up in business as a personal trainer, Adam immediately signs up to the programme – much to Pete's chagrin.

The adoption hits an obstacle. Adam and Rachel tell Ruth their good news – but she's not so delighted. This changes things, she says, and leaves to consult with

Kindred spirits. Karen finds Mark
hard to resist.

Jo's exercise class.

her superiors about the best way to proceed. She returns with bad news. The social workers feel that it would not be in Laura's best interests to be in a home with a new baby; when she was living at home, she was rejected after her mother gave birth to a child by a new partner. Laura needs stability and attention, which Ruth feels she won't get with Adam and Rachel. They're furious, and Ruth walks out of a painful meeting to cry in her car.

But Adam and Rachel aren't going to let it drop. They're convinced that they are the right parents for Laura, that they can give her all the love she needs even with a new brother or sister on the way. They consult a solicitor with a view to appealing against the decision, and he tells them some hard facts. The case is likely to drag on for months, it will cost them something in the region of £20,000 and they have a very poor chance of winning. Sadly and reluctantly, they agree to let Laura go.

Karen goes for dinner with Mark and his wife, Geraldine – who, it turns out, is the author of the lifestyle book she's been editing. Karen makes a few editorial suggestions which Geraldine flatly turns down; there's instant hostility between the two of them. This just makes things harder for Karen, who realises that her pleasure in working with Mark is not entirely due to professional satisfaction. She's falling in love with him – and when they discover that they're both recovering alcoholics, that just draws them closer together.

Pete and David are Jo's first personal trainees; Adam's out of the picture after
Rachel gets rushed into hospital with pains in her stomach that turn out to be
nothing more than wind. And soon, Pete and David are feeling the pain. After a
short run, Pete's puking up and David's feet are bleeding thanks to his very
expensive trainers. Jo's despondent; she feels that she's failed as a trainer. Pete
encourages her, though, and gets her a job as an aerobics instructor at his place
of work. Jo can't understand why Pete's being so nice to her – and Pete can't tell
her that he's fallen in love. He just assumes that she's way out of his league, and
when she starts dating one of his colleagues, Suggs, whom she's met at aerobics,
it confirms all his worst suspicions. His self-esteem hits an all-time low.

David hobbles home from the aerobics class complaining of terrible muscular
pain, which Karen relieves with a massage. And, for the first time in many months,
they kiss.

Goodbye

It's fitting that the final series of *Cold Feet* started at the airport, always a venue for poignant farewells.

Goodbye

Poor Pete. Both of the women he loved left him high and dry. First Jenny...

Goodbye

And then Jo.

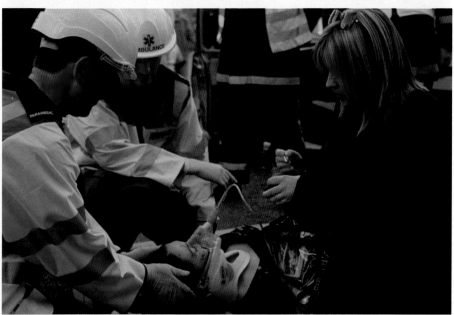

But the saddest farewell of all came as a shocking blow. Adam lost his Rachel.

Goodbye

Matthew lost his mother... and everyone else lost their dearest friend.

(top) The *Cold Feet* cast and crew hard at work.
(bottom) Pity James Nesbitt in his underpants on a cold, wet Manchester day.

It's harder to have sympathy for the crew at Pete and Jo's wedding.
Nice work if you can get it!

Thank you and goodbye from cast and crew.

Episode 6

Rachel's away and Adam's determined to play... David's bought a horse... Karen and Mark grow closer... so do Pete and Jo.

Rachel's Holiday

♡ Rachel went to New York in this episode; Helen Baxendale did not. She was heavily pregnant, and took a holiday (the episode was filmed in July; she had her baby in the October). And so Adam has the chance to indulge his taste for poker nights and women in sports cars...

While the cat's away, the mouse will play. Rachel's gone to New York to visit Jenny, and Adam realises that this is his last chance to have some fun before the realities of parenthood kick in. He's seen what's happened to his friends when they've become fathers – and he's determined to have one final fling. And so he organises a poker school...

Poker seems to bring out the worst in Adam Williams. All his less attractive characteristics – arrogance, bullying, aggression – come out in full force, while the rest of the players become rapidly disenchanted with what they thought was going to be a pleasant and social cards evening. Adam's obsessed by winning, but at the end of the night he's left on his own with a pile of pennies. That wasn't quite as much fun as he thought it would be.

David has had one of his bright ideas: he's bought Karen a race horse for her birthday. Of course, the present is really for him; Karen's not much interested in horses, whereas David is very impressed by the whole idea, and starts planning to entertain friends and clients at the races. This turns out to be a rather expensive hobby, as the stabling fees are £200 a week – David had assumed that figure was for a month. He starts scrabbling around for ways to offset the costs, but even his employers aren't interested in buying a race horse – so it looks as if David will have to bear the costs by himself.

For Karen, this is a minor distraction from the real matter in hand. She's working long into the night with Mark on his wife's book, and the two of them are becoming closer and closer. David comes home one night to find them still up, still working, still flirting... He's not happy with this interloper, but he has to trust Karen, especially now.

Pete is falling more and more in love with Jo, but it seems hopeless. She's still dating Suggs; Pete can't get a look-in. Jo agrees to help him out, and tries to coach him in a few basic dating skills: talking about films, for instance, is a great way of

One last fling for Adam.

finding out about someone, finding out if you have anything in common. It turns out that Jo and Pete have a lot in common: they both love Jeff Goldblum's Between the Lines, for instance. They certainly have more in common than Pete has with Liz, a colleague of Jo's that she tries to set him up with. And it seems that Jo has more in common with Pete than she does with Suggs... For the first time, she begins to wonder if she's going out with the wrong man.

Pete's bought himself a nice little MG soft-top to cheer himself up, and Adam can't wait to get his hands on it. But Pete won't let him. So Adam simply helps himself: he 'borrows' the spare keys and takes the car out for a spin, fantasising that he's 'Max Trendi', a James Bond figure with irresistible appeal to women. Fantasy swiftly turns to reality when he finds himself in a race through central Manchester with an attractive woman driving a BMW. She leads him back to her flat where, after several drinks, they go to bed.

Pete, meanwhile, has reported the theft of his car to the police. He's out for a drink with Jo, but his mind's on his car... And then, miraculously, he finds it

Jo bites the bullet and asks Pete out
on a date.

parked outside an apartment block. He has his keys in his pocket, so he drives it home. Adam, creeping guiltily from Deborah's house, discovers that the MG has disappeared. It's the end of a disastrous evening – he couldn't perform sexually with Deborah, but feels guilty anyway – and he has to report the theft to the police. This, inevitably, leads to Pete's mistaken arrest for stealing his own car.

Karen and Mark finally finish work on the book, and to celebrate Mark gives her a beautiful, expensive necklace. This, surely, is more than just a gift from a publisher to an editor. Karen confronts Mark on the real meaning of the present – and she doesn't get the answer she was expecting. Mark wants her to come and work for him full time. The jewellery was just a sweetener. It's an attractive idea, and Karen promises to think about it. When she gets home to bed, she makes love to David – but it's Mark she's thinking of. She realises where this is leading, and decides to turn down the job offer. It's just too dangerous.

David's organised a big day out for all his friends at the Chester race course. Karen's horse, Lady Perfect, is in the running, and he's hoping to make a good deal of money on her. But that's not the only drama at the races. Mark turns up and tells Karen he's fallen in love with her. 'Max' runs into Deborah, who embarrasses him in front of Pete. And Jo announces to Pete that she's chucked Suggs and would like to take him on a date.

Karen is flustered by Mark's declaration, and reaches for a glass of champagne. He stops her from drinking, there's a moment of deep understanding between them – and they kiss.

Lady Perfect, after a promising start, goes lame and loses the race.

'No offence, but I don't think you're going to reach.'

Rachel calms Adam's fears about sex during pregnancy

Episode 7

Rachel's back... and she's grown... Jo and Pete are getting closer and closer, but why won't he sleep with her?...Karen and Mark have no such problems...David gets promoted.

Rachel gets home from New York with one thing on her mind: sex. But for once, Adam's not up for it: Rachel's bump is getting big now, and he feels very uncomfortable with the idea of having sex with her in that condition. He tries to throw her off the trail by bringing up discussions of the baby's name at the most inappropriate moments – and this is not making Rachel a happy girl. She can't understand why Adam is so tense and jumpy; little does she know what he got up to while she was in America.

Karen has changed her mind about the job; her attraction to Mark is just so strong that she can't fight it. And David isn't showing himself at his best just now. He's under pressure from Natalie at work to make a few redundancies, and he's finding it difficult. Now he's back home, he just seems to be slipping back into old, bad habits, and Karen finds herself more interested in the alternatives. Mark, sensing that she's coming round, invites her out for lunch at the Buccina – a very nice restaurant that also happens to be a very nice hotel.

Waiting for him at the entrance, Karen sees Rachel approaching and uses this as her escape route. She drags Rachel off to the nearest café and confesses all: she's falling in love, she's putting her marriage on the line, she doesn't know what to do. Rachel seems to have forgotten that David very recently saved her marriage to Adam, and counsels Karen to follow her heart. She hasn't been happy for some time, it seems to Rachel, and Karen confesses that she's started to think she married the wrong person. And so she goes back to the Buccina, where Mark is waiting for her. They have lunch, and Mark has booked a room...

Pete and Jo are getting on nicely together. After their first date at the cinema, they've gone go-karting, and it's a lot of fun. Pete's delighted to have found a woman that shares his interests and his sense of humour, and Jo's thrilled to have found a man who actually cares about her. The only problem is the sex. Every time they get into a clinch, Pete applies the brakes. He says he doesn't want to rush into anything too quickly, but the truth of the matter is that he fears Jo will reject him when she sees him without his clothes on. Jo's perplexed; she can't understand why Pete keeps pushing her away, and starts to think that he just doesn't fancy her. This is bad news, because she has a history of relationships with

Jo gives up on Pete.

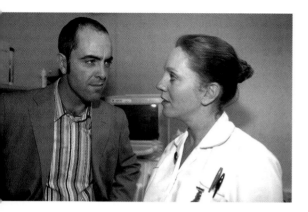

It's a boy! Adam sneaks
back to find out the sex.

commitment-phobic men.
Her last serious boyfriend in
Australia kept putting off
their marriage until Jo,
frustrated, ended the
relationship and came to
England to get away from
him. And now, once again,
she's found a man that she likes who doesn't want to know. When she gets a
letter from the Home Office informing her that her visa has run out, she decides
there's nothing to keep her in England and she might as well go home again.

Adam and Rachel are finding the late stages of pregnancy extremely stressful.
They're still not having sex, and they can't agree whether or not the child should
take its father's surname. Adam's obsessed by the idea of finding out what sex
the baby is, and Rachel doesn't want to know. Desperate, he goes behind her
back, asks the nurse and finds out he's expecting a son. Yet another row blows
up, and once again they are not on speaking terms. Finally a compromise is
reached: Rachel chooses the child's name – Matthew, after her grandfather.

Karen's affair has swiftly spiralled out of control. After that first afternoon in
the hotel, she and Mark are having sex at every available opportunity – including
in the office when the secretary has gone home. This nearly leads to disaster
when Karen accidentally punches a button on the telephone and leaves a
message (mostly grunts) on her answering machine at home. David just
dismisses it as a nuisance call, and erases it.

But she's in for one hell of a reality check. At the launch of Geraldine's book,
Mark's wife takes her to one side and says she knows what's going on, that Mark's
had many affairs before and that Karen's just the latest in a long line. When she
confronts Mark with his discovery, he tells her that she's the only one he's ever
really loved – and that he's prepared to leave his wife for her.

David executes a major blunder at work by accidentally emailing the entire
office with a confidential list of possible redundancies. The whole situation seems
about to blow up in his face, but his boss, Sir Donald, actually admires David's
style and gives him a promotion. It's Natalie's job – and as her parting gift to
David she gives him a bag containing 30 pieces of silver.

Pete realises, too late, that Jo really liked him after all; she'd told Rachel that
she was in love with Pete but he didn't fancy her. It seems that luck has once
again played a cruel trick on Pete Gifford – but, for once, he takes the bull by the

'Love makes liars of us all.'

Karen

horns and flies to Australia in hot pursuit. Adam and Rachel are woken up in the middle of the night by a telephone call from Sydney. It's Pete, telling them that things have worked out and he's back with Jo.

A few minutes later, the phone rings again. Jo has just asked Pete to marry her, and he wanted Adam to be the first to know.

Jo asks Pete to marry her. How can he refuse?

Episode 8

Everyone's in Australia... Karen chooses David and dumps Mark... Will Pete and Jo ever make it to the altar?... Adam and Rachel get a nasty surprise... Mark turns up.

Australia, here we come! Pete's getting married, and so the entire gang is flying to Sydney to celebrate. Karen and David are flying first class, or at least they were until Karen persuades David to give up his seat to a heavily-pregnant Rachel, who's booked into economy.

They're greeted at Sydney by the sight of Pete in full Australian costume, complete with a hat with corks dangling from it. He and Jo are on cloud nine, and can't wait for the wedding. Little do they know how many hoops they'll have to jump through before the happy day...

David has a surprise for Karen: he's booked her into a wonderful hotel with a view of Sydney Harbour, he's got tickets for Madam Butterfly (her favourite opera) and he's bought her a beautiful, and very expensive, necklace. The gesture doesn't go unnoticed, and when Karen seems in a receptive mood David pours out his heart to her, telling her how much he loves her and how desperate he is to start a new life together. If she can only put the past behind her and forgive his infidelity, learn to trust him again... Karen can say nothing, but she realises that it's time to make a choice. And so she emails Mark back in England to tell him that it's over.

David and Karen try again.

Jo's invited everyone over to spend some time at her father's house: it's an impressive set-up, with a pool, and soon everyone has stripped off and jumped in for a spot of skinny-dipping. This comes as some surprise to Rod, Jo's father, who arrives home unexpectedly from a business trip to find his pool full of naked people. And, it turns out, he knew nothing of the impending wedding. Meeting his future son-in-law for

the first time with a beach-ball concealing his genitals does not get the relationship off to the best start. Rod's convinced that Pete's just a gold digger, that he's only after Jo for her money, and he attempts to buy Pete off with a substantial offer of money. Pete's horrified, and tells Rod exactly where he can stick his money.

But Rod's a determined man, and he enlists Adam's help in derailing the marriage. Adam's gullible; he interprets Rod's doubts as real concern, and asks Pete whether he's sure he's doing the right thing in rushing into marriage with Jo. Pete flies off the handle; if that's the way Adam feels, then he needn't be best man.

Rachel's met up with her sister Lucy, who left England to live in Australia because she couldn't face the prospect of telling their father that she was a lesbian. Now she wants to have a child, and is looking for the right man to be its father. Rachel is horrified to learn that Adam has volunteered: not to have sex with Lucy, which even he would draw the line at (although she is very attractive), but to donate some of the sperm he banked when he had cancer. Eventually Rachel persuades Adam that this might not be such a great idea.

David has a plan. Karen seems to love Sydney so much that he believes they could start a new life out there with the children, and so he starts plotting secretly to secure a job with his firm's Sydney office. This involves leaving Karen to her own devices for a great deal of time, while David engineers a deal between his firm and Jo's father, a successful and wealthy builder. Karen doesn't mind too much: she has other fish to fry. Mark has turned up in Sydney, determined not to take no for an answer. He's left his wife, and he wants Karen. Faced with a choice, Karen chooses Mark. David's been neglecting her (obviously the memory of Madam Butterfly has faded quickly) and seems to be married only to his work. She can't face a future like that... so all that remains is to inform David of her decision.

Pete and Jo are having problems. Rod and Adam have sown doubt in his mind. Does he really know Jo well enough to marry her? And has he truly got over Jenny, or is this just a rebound relationship? When he finds himself accidentally referring to Jo and 'Jen', he realises he's in trouble and suggests that they should postpone the marriage. This is not what Jo wanted to hear: she's got troubles of her own, with her ex-fiance Shawn sniffing around telling her that he still loves her. It seems, after all, that Rod will get his way and the marriage will be cancelled.

David and Mark come to blows.

Adam realises that he's made a mistake; Jo really does love Pete, and Pete loves Jo, and external forces are driving them apart. So he persuades Rod to give the couple his blessing; Pete, says Adam, is the best man a woman could hope to marry, and if he loses Jo it will be the end of him. Rod realises that Adam's right, and so he brings the couple back together and gives them their wedding present – a penthouse in one of his new developments. He also agrees to a deal with David's firm – and the Sydney job seems to be in the bag.

David races home to tell Karen the good news: there's nothing to stand between them and a new life in

A happy ending for Pete and Jo. But
what about Karen and David?

Australia. But then he notices that Mark's there, that the atmosphere is strained. Mark, goaded by Karen's silence, blurts out the truth. He and Karen love each other, and she's leaving David. The two men are soon rolling on the floor punching each other's lights out, and David turns up to the wedding with a bleeding mouth.

On her way to the wedding, Rachel doubles up in agony and starts bleeding. This can't be right: she's still got two months to go, and it looks as if she's going to lose the baby. Adam rushes her to hospital where she has an emergency caesarean – and the baby is born, premature but healthy. It's a boy – but Adam already knew that.

Pete and Jo finally marry. David stands in as best man, and uses his and Karen's wedding rings to replace the ones that are still in Adam's pocket. And so Pete and Jo go on honeymoon, Adam and Rachel hold the child that they never believed they would have, and David returns to England... alone.

SC. 108. EXT.
STRICKLAND HOUSE. DAY.

ROD KISSES JO. THE WEDDING GUESTS APPLAUD.

JO: I love you Dad.

ROD: And I love you.

ROD SHAKES PETE'S HAND. THEN PETE GIVES HIM A BEAR HUG.

ROD: You take care of her now.

PETE TURNS TO JO AND SCOOPS HER UP IN HIS ARMS, CARRYING
HER OVER TO A SPEED BOAT IDLING AT THE JETTY. THE GUESTS
WATCH FROM THE SHORE. PETE AND JO KISS THEN STAND ON THE
BACK OF THE BOAT WAVING AS IT PULLS AWAY. JO THROWS HER
WEDDING BOUQUET. TO THE AMUSEMENT OF THE GUESTS IT FALLS AT
THE EDGE OF THE WATER - THE FEMALE GUESTS RUN FOR IT. THE
GUESTS CHEER AND WAVE AS THE BOAT PULLS AWAY. STANDING
ALONE ON THE SHORE IS DAVID, LOOKING MISERABLE. AS THE BOAT
DISAPPEARS ACROSS THE HARBOUR AND THE GUESTS GO BACK TO
BOOZING, KAREN STEPS UP TO DAVID'S SIDE.

KAREN: David? David?

DAVID TURNS TO LOOK AT HER. HIS FACE IS A MASK.

DAVID: No, Karen. No more.

DAVID TURNS AND WALKS AWAY UP THE GRASS. KAREN WATCHES HIM
GO BUT DOESN'T ATTEMPT TO FOLLOW HIM. A COUPLE OF BEATS,
THEN MARK STEPS UP AND PUTS A SOLICITOUS HAND ON KAREN'S
ARM. KAREN SHRUGS IT OFF, AND HERSELF WALKS AWAY, IN THE
OPPOSITE DIRECTION TO DAVID. MARK LOOKS CONFUSED - HE
THOUGHT SHE HAD CHOSEN HIM.

FADE TO BLACK.

CUT TO
SC. 109. INT.
HOSPITAL. DAY.

A TINY BABY (THREE AND A HALF POUNDS OR SO) LIES IN AN
INCUBATOR. HIS NAME IS MARKED ON THE GLASS SIDE OF THE
INCUBATOR; IT'S CLEARLY LEGIBLE: MATTHEW SYDNEY WILLIAMS.
SEPARATED BY A GLASS SCREEN, PEERING DOWN TO LOOK AT HIM
ARE, IN ORDER, JO, PETE, ADAM, RACHEL, AND KAREN. ADAM AND
RACHEL HAVE THEIR ARMS ROUND EACH OTHER. KAREN CAN'T ESCAPE
HER OWN UNHAPPINESS BUT IS DELIGHTED FOR ADAM AND RACHEL.

JO: He's so tiny!

PETE: I bet he's got massive bollocks.

JO ELBOWS PETE PLAYFULLY. HE GRINS AND PUTS HIS ARM ROUND
HER.

KAREN: He's absolutely beautiful.

RACHEL LOOKS AT KAREN AND SMILES GRATEFULLY.

JO: So the doctors say he's all right?

RACHEL: Yeah.

ADAM: He's perfect.

RACHEL: Though he's got to be kept in for three weeks. Just to be sure.

PETE: Oh great! That means you'll still be here when we get back from our honeymoon.

ADAM: I'll have the beers on ice.

PETE: Well we'll see you then.

ADAM: Peter, you can count on it.

As Adam and Pete banter, Rachel is conscious of Karen standing next to her on her own. Rachel looks at her sympathetically. Karen smiles bravely, but can't hide her desolation.

CUT TO
SC. 110. INT. AIRPLANE. DAY

BUSINESS CLASS. DAVID SITS ALONE IN A WINDOW SEAT. THE AISLE SEAT NEXT TO HIM IS EMPTY. THE PLANE HAS NOT YET TAKEN OFF. A STEWARDESS APPEARS IN THE AISLE WITH A TRAY OF DRINKS: CHAMPAGNE AND ORANGE JUICES.

STEWARDESS: Would you like a drink, Mr Marsden? Champagne or orange.

DAVID LOOKS AT HER BLANKLY, THEN LAUGHS EMPTILY.

DAVID: Champagne. Thank you.

THE STEWARDESS PUTS SOME NUTS DOWN ON DAVID'S ARM REST.

STEWARDESS: You're fortunate. The flight's not full, so you won't have anyone sitting next to you.

DAVID STARTS BREAKING DOWN AS HE ANSWERS. HE TURNS AWAY PRETENDING HE'S LOOKING OUT OF THE WINDOW, SO THAT SHE WON'T SEE THE TEARS COME.

DAVID: Yes, I'm very fortunate.

FACING THE WINDOW, THE TEARS COME. DAVID'S BODY IS WRACKED BY SILENT SOBS. WE STAY ON DAVID, CRYING SILENTLY INTO THE WINDOW.

THE END

Pete Gifford

(John Thomson)

Life is very unkind to Pete Gifford. He's what the French would call *un pauvre type* – basically, everything that can go wrong does go wrong for him. He's unlucky in love, unlucky at games, just plain unlucky. Sometimes this can be funny, and it's easy to laugh at Pete. But as often as not, it's bordering on the tragic. Pete deals with it by putting on a brave face, being one of the lads and drowning his sorrows at the pub, but beneath the bluff exterior he's a sensitive little soul. Pete's life is a vicious circle: he tries something, gets knocked back, drinks, puts on weight, his self-esteem goes down, then he rallies himself and tries again. He's certainly an optimist, even though life has tried its hardest to teach him otherwise.

Pete is not an ambitious man. When Jenny says that the height of his ambition is a loft-conversion, she's not altogether wrong. He's content with the little things in life – not because he's a small person, but because he values simple things very highly. He hates and resists change, and that often means that the people who are close to him get frustrated. His marriage to Jenny suffers because he's not willing to accept that she has grown up and changed since they met at school. In Pete's eyes, they're eternal teenagers – so when Jenny starts to want different things, he gets scared. Instead of recognising this as part of growing up, he tries to block it out. Result: frustrated, unhappy wife, broken marriage.

Pete's misfortune is that he's attracted to people who are much more dynamic and outgoing than himself. Jenny was always the feisty one when they first went out, and she gave Pete a great deal of confidence. Adam, too, was popular, witty, a natural leader. And Jo, Pete's second wife, is an easy-going, confident young woman who slips easily into the dominant role. Pete's one of nature's second fiddles, and is, by and large, content with that role. Unfortunately for him, the people around him get frustrated by his lack of drive, and ultimately they outgrow him. Only Adam remains faithful to Pete – but that's because Adam needs someone to whom he can always feel superior. Their's is a real, true friendship, and they look out for each other – but there's a strong element of emotional S&M going on in there.

So what do all these lively, dynamic people see in Pete? It's not for nothing that Jenny, Adam and Jo like being around him, and it can't be just because he boosts their ego. The fact is that Pete is a truly decent man. He has a strong

> **'You're bound to get another bloke, Jenny. Top bird like you. That's if your body holds up.'**
>
> Pete Gifford, tactful as ever

MIKE BULLEN ON *Pete*

> Pete is everyone's best mate. He's not quite as attractive as Adam, not quite as quick-witted. He's the butt of all the jokes, and the cause of much laughter. That's a role he's become accustomed to, and he plays up to it because it makes him popular. Everyone loves Pete: he's solid and reliable. He's never going to set the world on fire; when Jenny says that the height of his ambition is a loft conversion, she's not far from the truth. Pete was actually based on my best mate Mark, whom I've known since I was 11, but I'd like to think that I've treated him a bit better than Adam treats Pete. I once went out with a girl that he'd had his eye on, and we didn't speak for six months, but that's how friends behave.

moral sense, he is incredibly loyal and he would always put himself out for a friend. This can lead to muddled priorities, and it's always frustrating for his partners when he rushes off to listen to Adam's latest problems. But, even when he's driving his women up the wall, they realise that he's trying to do the right thing. In addition to that, Pete's fun to be around. He has a great, dry, Mancunian sense of humour that sees the absurd in any situation. He's got a great line in repartee, even if, on occasion (his best man's speech at Adam and Rachel's wedding, for instance) it can go awry. Women like him because he makes them laugh, even though the joke is often at his own expense. Pete's not as physically attractive as Adam (and doesn't Adam like to remind him?), and he suffers from very low self-esteem when it comes to sex, but once he feels confident with a partner he's willing to give himself entirely to her.

Whatever his virtues, though, Pete just never seems able to get anything right. Take his relationship with his parents, for instance. He loves them, they love him, but he can't shake himself out of sulky adolescence, and does nothing but bicker with his father. He only realises he loves him when it's too late and his father is dead. That's typical of the pattern of Pete's relationships; his timing's always off, and he can never say what he thinks. When his mother comes back into his life, Pete instantly reverts to childhood, and lets her boss him around – even when it's Audrey that has come to him for help. Pete finds it hard to accept the responsibilities of adulthood, and there's a part of him that will always be a teenager.

His relationships with women are, basically, disastrous. He's always so surprised that a woman can find him attractive that he's instantly looking for problems. While Adam accepts adoration as his natural due, Pete is suspicious, always rooting out the ulterior motive. This is never more evident than in his relationship with Jo. Love comes slowly between the two of them, and she's not instantly attracted – but once she gets to know him, she truly loves him. That's not enough for Pete; as soon as the honeymoon's over, he's looking for the cracks. The suspicion that she might only have married him for a visa is enough to smash the whole thing to smithereens, and from there it's only a short step to discovering that she's been unfaithful to him. And so: game over.

Pete's real problem is that he never learns from his mistakes. He was unfaithful to Jenny, so he should know just how hard it is to remain monogamous in a long-term relationship. He knew it meant nothing, that he always loved Jenny – but as soon as anyone else is unfaithful to him, he's slamming doors and giving people their marching orders. He wants to be understanding and forgiving, and at his best he is – but those demons of self-doubt will always be prompting him to see the worst in any situation.

Pete faces the worst – the loss of his wife and child – and somehow survives. He messes up all his relationships, but somehow people stick by him and are always willing to help him out, despite his disgusting personal habits. Finally, he gets another chance with Jenny, a chance to recreate his family, to be a father to little Adam and to Jenny's second child. We can only hope that, this time round, he'll deal with things with a little more maturity. On past form, however, this doesn't seem likely. Give it six months?

Loves
♡ Jenny

♡ Going down the pub

♡ His friends

♡ Being a Dad

Hates
☺ Himself

☺ Golf

☺ Washing-up

☺ Infidelity

John Thomson

(Pete Gifford)

Little did he know it, but John Thomson had already auditioned for Cold Feet a year or so before the pilot was made. 'I was in a TV film called Perfect Match, with Con O'Neill and Saskia Reeves, that Mike Bullen had written, and basically the character that I was playing was an early version of Pete. So I was on board with Cold Feet from the beginning. I only discovered recently that the character was based on Bullen's best mate, so I can't wait to find out what that's really all about.'

In the pilot, Pete was a pretty feckless individual, batted between Adam and Jenny like a shuttlecock. 'We knew the pilot was good, and we thought that it had a lot of potential, but there are loads of TV projects that have potential that never get commissioned. To be honest, I wasn't sure if Cold Feet could really cut the mustard. But then we heard that it got the Golden Rose at Montreux. Things should have happened quickly after that, but Granada were a bit slow off the mark. It's hard to believe now, when we're constantly being told that it's ITV's flagship show, but very few people had faith in Cold Feet at the beginning, and it very nearly didn't get off the ground. It wasn't until the second series that anyone in ITV had faith in it. People are always asking me what's the secret of Cold Feet's success, and there's only one answer: word of mouth. People saw it, and they liked it. It didn't fit in with anything else, it wasn't like a normal comedy or a normal drama, but it worked. I think it kind of crept up on ITV. After the first two series, everyone was asking for the videos for Christmas, and then they all started watching series three. So ITV had this huge hit on their hands, and it had come out of nowhere.'

Thomson was already well established as a stand-up comedian and comic actor when Cold Feet gave him the opportunity to show off his dramatic talents. 'Up to that point, I was universally known as Fat Bob [Steve Coogan's sidekick in the Paul/Pauline Calf shows]. I was getting a bit fed up of it, really; it's not as if he was called Johnny Longhorn. So Cold Feet finally got me away from Large Robert, and people started shouting 'Oi! Pete!' at me in the street. In the first series, Pete was just a foil for Adam, really – his less successful, less attractive, less intelligent mate. He was a useful tool for Mike Bullen, because he was always there for Adam to bounce ideas off, or to discuss his problems over a drink. But when Pete's marriage started to collapse, he became a character in his own right. Jenny told Pete she didn't love him any more, and he became interesting. It was in the third series that I started to get really good material.'

It's on Thomson's shoulders that Cold Feet's mantle as a hard-partying show rests. 'It really was a non-stop party to start with. Jimmy Nesbitt and I were

partners in crime, real drinking buddies. It took a while, but by the second series we'd really bonded as mates and we just went for it. We spent the next two years making sure we'd eaten in every restaurant, and had a drink in every bar in Manchester – and that takes some doing, I can tell you. I spent so much time with Jimmy that I can now do a really mean impersonation of him. It's really useful. I can phone people up and leave messages in his voice, which is always a good way of causing trouble.'

Incredibly, both Nesbitt and Thomson worked consistently in between series of *Cold Feet*. 'At one point I was doing *Playing the Field*, *The Fast Show* and *Cold Feet* all at the same time. It was a nightmare. I don't know what I was thinking, because it's a really stupid way of running your life. You're living out of a bag, running from one hotel to another. I just had to get a really fast car so that I could race up to Nottingham to do *Playing the Field*, then to Manchester for *Cold Feet*, then to Newcastle for *The Fast Show*. And I was playing so many different characters in the space of a week, I started to develop some kind of multiple personality disorder. That was four years ago, and I learned my lesson. It's all to do with scheduling: you can't say yes to everything, however tempting it might be. Jimmy's the same: he likes to work all the time, but I think we've both reached the point when we have to look at our priorities and turn a few things down. I know for Jimmy that came when he had children – and now I've got a baby as well. That makes a big difference. I've calmed down a lot since meeting Sam (Thomson's partner), and being a father is another big step. It's exactly the same process that the *Cold Feet* characters go through, and that's one of the reasons we're so committed to the show. It's totally rooted in the reality of our lives.'

Not long after this, Pete and Jo were history.

That said, Thomson is still working as hard as ever. In the summer of 2002 he recorded the first series of ITV's *Stan the Man*, which adopted the *Cold Feet* crew and used some of the same sets. He also continued voicing the new series of *Bill and Ben*. 'There's a danger of being over-exposed, but if you get a job like *Stan the Man* you can't say no. There's a downside to it: of course you get over-exposed, and you start to get a lot of unwelcome attention from the media. To be honest, the press was absolute shit while we were making the last series of *Cold Feet*. They wouldn't leave me alone. It's ridiculous, because my work and my private life are totally separate things. I always behave myself in public; if someone comes over and asks nicely to have their picture taken with me, or for an autograph for their granddad, then I'm happy to oblige. But we got a lot of papparazzi who were pretending to be fans, who hung around set asking for pictures, and then when they discovered I wasn't there they lost interest. I think that's really low.'

Spencer Campbell

(PRODUCER)

Spencer Campbell has produced **Cold Feet** since the third series, when original producer Christine Langan moved up to an executive production role.

As such he's seen the show through its busiest times, managing the increase from six to eight episodes and organising the most complicated location trips – notably the Australian jaunt that finished off series four. 'That was a nightmare,' he says. 'We were trying to prepare for the trip while we were still filming in England, and the scripts were late so we didn't really know what exactly we were preparing for. The scripts are always late with Cold Feet, which adds a little extra excitement to each series, because without a script you can't brief a designer. The Australian trip had the added complication of having to hire a whole new crew, because we couldn't afford to fly the

'Cold Feet is big in Australia.'

usual Cold Feet crew over there and put them all up in hotels. So we were working with a strange crew, shooting scripts that we'd only just received, in a different country. It wasn't easy.'

To add to Campbell's problems, he had to accommodate the very real needs of certain cast members. 'Helen Baxendale was heavily pregnant at the

time, and she couldn't fly. But Rachel was going to Australia, and so we had to film all her scenes in Manchester as if they were in Sydney. All Rachel's scenes were interiors; you never saw her walking down a Sydney street. The airport scenes that she appears in were shot in Manchester Airport, not Sydney. Continuity was an absolute nightmare as a result. You had actors walking through a door in Manchester and emerging on to a street in Sydney, and we had to make sure that they were wearing the same clothes, with the same hair and skin tones, all the way through. Everything was packed up into body bags and shipped out: wardrobe, accessories, and lots of polaroids for reference.'

It was the Australian episode, the finale of Series Four, that won Cold Feet its Bafta – so Campbell and his team must have been doing something right. 'Cold Feet is big in Australia, so it made sense for us to film there. But a lot of shows that go to Australia end up being swamped by the place; it becomes about the country, about prawns on the barbie, rather than about the characters. We made a conscious decision just to film an ordinary episode of Cold Feet with a different background. It was true to

Spencer
Campbell
on location

itself and I think that's why it worked.'

This was to have been the last ever episode of *Cold Feet*; it had certainly been announced as such. 'I felt immense relief when it was decided to end the show after the fourth series,' says Campbell, 'because it was getting harder and harder keeping the stories going, let alone getting the actors back for another series. But as we made the fourth series, everyone got into it again, and we became so enthusiastic about the show that we realised there was the potential for one more series if we could get the team back together again. There are many reasons, though, why this is the last ever series. For one thing, Mike Bullen has definitely finished with it. He's moved to Australia and he's doing new things. We've tried out other writers on *Cold Feet*, and some of them have done a great job, but at the end of the day what you want when you watch *Cold Feet* is a Mike Bullen script. It's cost us thousands of pounds to realise that.

'The other factor is the cast. They all want to go off and do different things, and it's hard for them to commit to a project if they know that Cold Feet is going to take up half their year. And to be honest, we can't really afford them any more. Our overall budgets have gone up, but the cast takes up a much larger chunk of the money. We wanted to have a nice location trip to finish off the fifth series, but there's no way we could afford to go somewhere like Australia this time. So we had to settle for Port Meirion – and we had to fight to get that! But you have to give the show

'That's one of the things I like about Cold Feet: it's a very good-looking show.'

some production values; people have come to expect it. We've always had a nice location trip, and we didn't want to take that away for the final series. That's one of the things I like about Cold Feet: it's a very good-looking show, it's aspirational, the characters are well dressed and it looks filmic. Location spend is part of that. I'm proud of the fact that we've always given viewers a bit more for their money: they get flashbacks, fantasy sequences, great music and great

locations. It's a glossy show; a lot of our directors shoot expensive, glossy commercials, and they bring that visual style to Cold Feet. Viewers have come to understand that the show is not only funny and intellectually challenging, it's also a visual treat.'

A great part of Cold Feet's appeal lies in its presentation of a pleasure-seeking lifestyle. The characters may have problems and responsibilities, but they also spend a large part of their lives in nice restaurants and going on holiday. This phenomenon was not restricted to the screen; off-duty, the cast and crew were well known for their love of a party. 'Cold Feet used to be the party show,' says Campbell. 'There were a lot of people up here in Manchester, away from home, with nothing to do in the evenings, and so we all went out. During series four, we had a mid-production wrap party; we'd finished the first block of filming, and it seemed like a good excuse to celebrate. I'd very stupidly scheduled a read-through for the second block on the following morning. New cast members, like Victoria Smurfit who played Adam's ex-girlfriend Jane, were coming into the show, and of course they all turned up at 11am on the dot. The regulars came straggling in over the following hour with the most ginormous hangovers. Some of them actually had to have their pages turned over for them. Afterwards, I went along to apologise to Victoria Smurfit, who'd been working on *Ballykissangel* and was probably used to a more decorous style of behaviour. But she was pleased. She said "It just goes to show that rock & roll is not dead!"'

'It's quietened down a lot now, though. More of the cast have children, and we're all a bit older and a bit calmer. When they're not working on *Cold Feet*, the cast usually have other jobs, so they have to prepare for those. We still have a good time, and the final wrap party will be one to remember.'

As *Cold Feet* gained ever greater audiences, press interest grew to reflect its popularity. During the final series, the production was dogged by photographers and reporters from the tabloids, desperate to get a story on any of the cast members, but particularly John Thomson. 'Journalists picked up on *Cold Feet* pretty quickly, and realised that it was a phenomenon. First of all the coverage was pretty positive – they were really interested in the show and what it meant. But inevitably, the attention turned more and more towards the actors. We got our first taste of that in Australia, where the show is huge. There were paparazzi all over the place; *Cold Feet* coming to Sydney was a big story for the press over there. I

remember walking down the street with Robert and Hermione, and people were leaning out of windows screaming 'Leave him!' at her. The papers ran endless stories about the show, and it was long lenses everywhere we went. It never used to be like that at home, but it has been for the final series. The main interest now is the actors' private lives, not the show. *Cold Feet* made those actors into stars, and so I suppose they're now paying the price.'

'I can understand the interest; it's a

'Journalists picked up on Cold Feet pretty quickly.'

big show, and they're feeding a demand. Most of the time I don't mind, but sometimes they give away storylines, and I think that's out of order. We had photographers shooting in the crematorium when we were filming Rachel's funeral, and of course those photographs were published. They got their facts wrong, but it still gave a big storyline away and spoiled it for the audience. I try hard to maintain security when we're filming; I tell people not to leave scripts lying around, that sort of thing. But stories will leak. It's impossible to control the press any more.'

Karen's Other Men

Alexander Welch (Dennis Lawson)
Famous – or infamous – as the author of *Blanket of Tears*, Alexander Welch appeals to Karen both as an author and as a lover. He's charming, attentive and very appreciative of her professional expertise – three qualities in which David is spectacularly lacking. Inspired by Alec's obvious understanding of female sexuality (he did, after all, write 'that scene when she's ironing'), Karen starts to believe that she and her author are having some kind of affair. He touches her hand over lunch, he flatters her, and he even dedicates his new novel to her. In truth, it's in recognition of her skills as an editor, but Karen jumps to conclusions... When she accompanies Alec to Liverpool on a book signing, she decides that she's going to take the plunge, and turns up at his hotel room with a bottle of champagne – only to discover that Alec already has company. His understanding of female sexuality, it seems, is based on extensive research in the field, and Karen returns to Manchester with her tail between her legs.

Miles Brodie (Richard Dillane)
Miles Brodie is a reminder of Karen's wild youth. As students together, they organised protests, enjoyed riots and, inflamed by the heady wine of college politics, had regular sex. They even made love under the stage at a Rock Against Racism gig while the Stranglers were on stage. Now Miles is a successful photographer, and when Karen hears him on a radio show she decides to get back in touch. There's still a spark between them, which nearly kindles when Karen helps Miles to organise an exhibition of his photography – but Karen's not ready to play away from home. Not yet.

Mark Cubitt (Sean Pertwee)

Mark is everything that Karen is looking for in a man. He's attractive, wealthy and successful. Like her, he's in publishing. Like her, he's a recovering alcoholic. And, unfortunately, like her, he's married. But Karen is past caring about such details; David

cheated on her, and she's more than ready to cheat on him. The attraction to Mark is genuine enough, but for Karen he's the perfect antidote to adultery blues. Soon they're working together on a women's lifestyle book, written by Mark's wife, Geraldine – who instantly suspects that her husband is having an affair. She takes Karen aside and tries to warn her off, but to no avail; after a few more late nights over the proofs, Karen and Mark are lovers. Karen tries to resist, but it's no use. She chooses to ignore Geraldine's warning that Mark's a serial adulterer, that she's just another in a long line; it seems too real for that. The crunch comes, however, when Mark makes it clear that he wants Karen, but he's not interested in raising another man's children, and so Karen decides to end the relationship. But that's not enough for Mark, who follows her out to Australia and forces her to choose between him and David. Karen makes her choice – or so it seems. In the event she can't make up her mind between the devil and the deep blue sea – and when she finally does decide to go back to David, it's too late. He's with Robyn, and Karen's left alone.

'I love you. I can't love your children.'

Mark burns his bridges with Karen

Rachel Bradley

(HELEN BAXENDALE)

How do you solve a problem like Rachel Bradley? How do you catch a wave upon the sand? Rachel's like quicksilver; no sooner do you think you know her than she's changed again. That's one of the reasons why Adam loves her, and why her friends always look out for her: there's something slightly dangerous and exciting about Rachel. Men find that an irresistibly attractive quality – that and the fact that Rachel is drop-dead gorgeous. Women find it endearing and enviable. As long as Rachel's around, something exciting is bound to happen. Exciting doesn't always mean good, and in her time Rachel's caused everyone some hideous problems. But she's certainly never boring.

Rachel's a curious combination. In some ways she's a femme fatale: she can be cruel and entirely selfish, using her sexuality to exercise power over men. On the other hand, she's almost entirely unconscious of the effect she's having on people. At heart she's just a sweet-natured girl who likes to have fun and enjoys the attention of others – but she's always getting herself into trouble. That's partly because men are always coming on to her, and sometimes it's very hard to resist temptation. But she also has a knack for doing or saying the wrong thing. For those who know her well, Rachel's bombshells are a way of life. To outsiders, they can seem insensitive or downright cruel.

'I was married. I was pregnant, didn't know who the father was. I had an abortion. Adam and I can't have children. Oh, yes. Your younger daughter — she's a lesbian.'

A Rachel bombshell drops in her parents' laps

In many ways, Rachel is the most forward-looking and liberated of the *Cold Feet* women. She's always regarded herself as an equal in any relationship with a man, and she's had her fair share of wild times and one night stands; she's been a bit of a "ladette" in her time. And she's never fallen into the trap of conventionality like Karen has. Rachel would never settle for a marriage like Karen's: she'd be far too aware of its limitations. She's professionally ambitious and successful in a way that leaves Jenny standing. And throughout her relationship with Adam, she's quick to spot any attempt at male-chauvinist-piggery. This matters to her, and not just in the little things. She'll argue about whether or not their child will take his name or hers, but ultimately they both realise that a compromise is the best solution. But there are other, bigger areas

All she ever wanted: a baby and Adam.

in which Rachel will stand her ground: her right to independence, the validity of her opinions, her sexual needs. She's escaped the traditional constrictions of her sex, and will never settle for less than absolute equality.

For all that, Rachel's a very girly girl. She's disorganised to the point of distraction, she's fluffy in her thinking, she's easily won over by compliments and flirting. She can also be monumentally selfish – albeit for the best possible motives. Whenever she sees her parents, she insists on raking up their unhappy past, and will never forgive her father for hitting her mother. Perhaps she's right: spousal abuse is a hideous thing, hard to forgive. But she's completely unaware that her morally upright stance is simply causing her mother more pain. And she thinks nothing of outing her own sister just as a way of proving her moral superiority to her parents. When her sister manages to patch things up with the family, Rachel feels personally affronted – how can they be getting along when she's still out on a limb? It's a form of stubbornness that manifests itself in all areas of Rachel's life.

One of the most revealing episodes in Rachel's life concerns the fall-out from her first marriage, to Kris. She's never told her friends about it, and she's certainly never mentioned it to Adam. It was something that didn't go right in Rachel's life, and she's not used to that, so she prefers to

Loves

♡ Having fun

♡ Having sex

♡ Children

♡ Adam

Hates

⊚ Conventionality

⊚ Male chauvinists

⊚ Her Dad

⊚ Inequality

keep it hidden. And instead of divorcing Kris when the matter arises, she prefers to keep her options open – not an attractive trait. She did the same with Simon, her boyfriend before Adam; as soon as a man says he loves her Rachel finds it impossible to say no. When Kris comes back into her life, as attractive as ever and repenting his past misdeeds, Rachel's commitment to Adam suddenly goes out the window and she sleeps with him. It's easy to blame the booze, but the fact remains that her own high standards have been fatally compromised.

When it turns out that she's pregnant by an unknown father, Rachel's response is typically extreme. Instead of staying with the man who really loves her, she turns her back on the whole sorry situation and runs away to London, then decides, on her own, to terminate the pregnancy. Depending on your personal beliefs, this could either be an act of admirable self-reliance, or an example of appalling selfishness. Either way, it doesn't stop Adam from loving her

Rachel's bumpy existence is buoyed up by the fact that she's always going to have plentiful admirers. If one relationship goes wrong, another one will be along in a minute. In Adam, she meets her match; and through their trials and tribulations, they learn that they can only find true happiness through commitment to one long-term partner. It's Rachel's tragedy that she only finds this out in time for her final appointment with a speeding lorry.

MIKE BULLEN ON Rachel

Rachel is the only character in **Cold Feet** who isn't based on a real person. She's more an amalgam of qualities of my fantasy ideal girlfriend. She started out as a rather vague person, and gradually the character was influenced by the actor. Helen Baxendale is very attractive, in a girl-next-door way, and that's what Rachel became. She can be a bit ditsy, a bit tactless, but without malice. She's away with the fairies a lot of the time. She's done some pretty awful things over the years — the abortion, particularly — and in someone else that might be unforgiveable. But you tend to forgive Rachel because she's so sweet and lovely and you seem to sympathise with her predicament. At first I always had the impression that Adam loved Rachel more than Rachel loved Adam, but as the show went on they became much more equal. By the end they're indissoluble.

Adam loses the girl he met in the car park.

Helen with the Golden Rose of Montreux.

Cold Feet

Helen Baxendale

(Rachel Bradley)

Helen Baxendale admits to having been 'absolutely terrified' at the prospect of playing Rachel Bradley. 'Most of the TV work I'd done up to that point was pretty straight; I hadn't really done much comedy, and I was very frightened of it. The main thing I learned over five years of doing Cold Feet is not to worry about being funny – I'm not a comedian, so I just had to learn to relax and play the part and give a good performance, and rely on the writing and the situations to get the laughs.'

This is a little too modest: in fact, Baxendale had already carved out a neat line in gallows humour in the BBC hospital drama Cardiac Arrest, in which she played superbitch doctor Claire Maitland. 'But that was different. It was so dark and shocking that the situations got the laughs. I didn't have to be funny; the humour came from the subject matter. In Cold Feet it's all about characters, and I never felt that Rachel was a particularly funny character. Over the years I found a way of playing her that drew on aspects of my own character which seemed to work pretty well; I found something quirky in myself, which became part of Rachel. But it was a long process. Usually when you play a role, you see the character in the script and you grasp on to that; your whole performance is based round a clearly-drawn set of qualities. But Rachel didn't have that, and I had to learn to draw on myself.'

Mike Bullen is the first to admit that Rachel was, initially, the least realistic and least rounded of the Cold Feet characters, being little more than a projection of his own ideal girlfriend. 'To start off with, Rachel was just "the girlfriend",' says Baxendale. 'She wasn't a real woman with a life of her own; she was just the woman that Adam wanted to have a relationship with. She was the love interest, and that's both limiting and bloody hard to play. Over the years she's developed into a real person, and that's much easier. But at first she was just someone that Adam saw through rose-tinted glasses. She didn't have a life of her own, and viewers didn't know what to make of her. That's because I didn't know what to make of her. I think as time went on, the writers started to give her more of a personality, and allowed her to make decisions for herself, and from that point on Mike Bullen had a clearer idea of who Rachel was and how to write for her.'

Over five series of Cold Feet, Rachel has had more than her fair share of dramas. She's won Adam, lost Adam and won him back on a regular basis. She's revealed a secret husband, had an affair with him, conceived a baby (possibly his) and terminated the pregnancy. She's discovered that she's infertile, gone through the agony of adoption only to have the child taken away from her, then conceived her own baby despite the odds. Then, to cap it all, she gets killed in a

The story of friendship is integral to *Cold Feet*

road accident. 'I do think that it's terribly unfair, what happens to Rachel,' says Baxendale. 'I don't really know what she's being punished for. I know that she had an affair with her ex while she was going out with Adam, but all the characters do things like that, so I don't see why Rachel has to be singled out for special punishment. It's like divine retribution for some terrible sin. Yes, she terminated her pregnancy, but she was in a very difficult situation at the time. She was on her own, and she did what she thought was right. I would prefer people to feel sympathy for her; after all, millions of women have abortions. But instead Rachel was punished with infertility and death. But of course, drama must be drama, and there wouldn't be much of a story if these bad things didn't happen.'

For many audiences, the core of *Cold Feet* was the love story between Adam and Rachel – and that's certainly been the focal point for Baxendale. 'When we were shooting the final series, Jimmy [Nesbitt] said to me "I can't stand it, Helen – I've been married to you for all these years and now you're dead!" I said "Jimmy... it's not real...", but I could see his point. It's like having a husband that I come back to from time to time, and it's become very real, to the point where I feel I know Jimmy very well. I've never had sex with him, obviously, but other than that it is very much like being married.'

The climax of the fifth series means, of course, that this is the end of the line for Adam and Rachel; there's no chance of another series. 'It's right that it should end now, because all the characters have done everything to everyone else, and it would start to get a bit bonkers. Adam and Rachel have gone through every permutation of a relationship, and I think it would run out of steam. From my point of view, the show was always at its best when Adam and Rachel were just having a normal relationship, when they were dealing with the ups and downs of life together. When they were apart, I felt it lost something, and audiences always wanted them to be together. They didn't make a lot of sense as separate individuals. So the final episode is unbearably sad. It's a real tragedy: Adam loses the girl that he met in the car park. I was really upset that they killed Rachel off

Helen becomes Rachel.

– not because I don't want the series to end, because it's happened at a good time for me, but because I think people will be terribly upset. Rachel's been brutally treated. Thank you, Mike Bullen!'

Life's changed a good deal for Helen Baxendale in the last seven years – not least because she's now got two school-age children. 'My whole outlook on work is different now. When I first did *Cold Feet*, I was up for just about anything, and I wanted to get as much work under my belt as I could. But now my priorities are my children and my family life. *Cold Feet* has been a great job for me because it's enabled me to earn my money in about four months, and spend the rest of the time at home. I've been able to bring the family up to Manchester when we're filming here, and they've come on trips with me. My daughter took her first steps when we were filming in Lindisfarne. But there comes a point when I'm ready to move on; the series is ending at the right time for me. I want to be a hands-on mother.'

So with the death of Rachel, Helen's going to spend some time focussing on her family and plotting her next move. She's not sure where her future lies, but after several years playing the sam character, she's pretty certain that she's done her sting of long-running TV dramas. 'I've loved *Cold Feet*, but I've disrupted my children's lives enough by dragging them up to Manchester for months at a time. I feel so guilty about it and now I think it's time I took on some more varied roles which perhaps don't take up so much time.'

She's also discovered that being in a successful long-running TV show has its draw-backs. *Cold Feet* was always a joy and nothing but a joy. But in the middle of that I did three months on *Friends* [As Ross's English love-interest Emily]. The amount of press intrusion into my life was ridiculous. We've had a certain amount of unwelcome press attention on *Cold Feet*, but it was nothing compared to *Friends*. The pressure was intense, and I don't think I ever want to be that famous again. I really distrust the culture of celebrity, all the papers and magazines. It really upsets me that our culture is going that way, that young people think that's all that matters in life. It's inane.

Helen Baxendale is not disappearing, however. She made a few low-profile films that will come out after the fifth series of *Cold Feet*, and she'[s still reading scripts. 'I went into acting because I loved the variety and interest that playing lots of different roles can bring and even though *Cold Feet* was a fantastic experience, I'm ready for a new challenge now.'

Pete's Other Women

Amy (Rosie Cavliero)

Amy starts off as a sexually available colleague of Pete's who gets set up with Adam on a blind date. It soon becomes clear that Amy is a woman of prodigious sexual appetites. As soon as Rachel's back on the scene, Adam dumps Amy. Pete takes pity on her, and a new friendship develops – just in time for Pete to be dumped by Jenny. And so, in a remote Travelodge during an Outward Bound course, Pete and Amy become lovers. The affair continues back in Manchester, even though Pete is 'officially' getting back together with Jenny. Eventually Jenny confronts the guilty lovers. It's too much for Amy, who realises that Pete's priorities lie elsewhere, and she leaves Manchester for Bristol.

Emma (Pooky Quesnel)

Pete thinks he's on to a winner when he starts an online flirtation with a woman called "Girlpower". She's really a teacher, name of Brenda Heeve, and Pete dutifully goes to

meet her at school only to discover that he's been the stooge in a class experiment, that Brenda Heeve does not exist and is in fact only an anagram (Ever Been Had?). But Emma, the class teacher, is very real indeed, and is a very welcome consolation prize. Eventually Pete finishes with Emma and gets back with his wife - but not for long.

Parents

Algernon and Audrey Gifford
(Sam Kelly and Doreen Keogh)

Pete doesn't get on with his Dad. They're far too similar; they argue about trivial things, and disguise the fact that they really love each other under a mask of masculine indifference. Things come to a head over the naming of Pete's son; his father wants the traditional Algernon name to continue in the Gifford line. Pete refuses to inflict it on his son, and the pair part on non-speaking terms. Pete realises, too late, just what his father really felt about him, as Gifford Senior dies of a heart attack during the christening.

Audrey is another thorn in Pete's flesh, the typical, interfering mother who can't accept the fact that her son has grown up. She arrives at Pete and Jenny's house and immediately tries to take over; it's her way of showing that she loves them, but it doesn't go down well with Jenny, who nearly stabs Audrey with a kitchen knife. The two women realise, quickly, how similar they are, and a bloodbath is averted. Widowed after Algernon's death, Audrey reappears in Pete's life when he's got David lodging with him, and it soon becomes apparent that she's losing her marbles. A nasty incident with a chip pan convinces her to seek sheltered accommodation. After a few teething troubles, she finds a place that she likes – and she finds an unexpected cure for her insomnia. We last see Audrey as an unlikely drug dealer in an old people's home.

Heather (Mel Martin)

Heather is an awful warning to her daughter: she's exactly the kind of woman that Karen could become if she doesn't watch her step. She and Karen's father have moved out to Spain, where they live the ex-pat lifestyle, all rhino-hide tans and all-day happy hour. When she turns up at the Marsdens' to lend a hand with the twins, it soon becomes apparent that there's another reason for her sudden departure from Spain. She's left Karen's father, she says, and she's relocating to England, drink problem and all. At first it seems she'll make a go of it – she starts dating David's colleague Felix, and gains a measure of independence. But Felix turns out to be a bad lot (he tries to get Heather to "swing"), and she realises that, after all, her place is at her husband's side - much to Karen's relief.

Bill (Ian Mcelhinney)

We know little of Adam's background until the very end of Cold Feet, when we learn that his father, Bill, walked out when Adam was just a kid, and has never had any further contact with him. This was the great shadow over Adam's early life, and explains a lot of his attention-seeking behaviour. When Bill shows up again to try and form a relationship with his new grandson, Adam's having none of it – and it takes Rachel to discover the real reason why Bill left. Finally Bill gets a chance to explain things to Adam: he left his wife for another man, and Adam's mother would never allow him to have any contact with his son after that. Adam realises that he's misjudged his father – and, in the aftermath of Rachel's death, it's to Bill that he turns for support.

Mary and Brian Bradley
(Sue Holderness and Paul Ridley)
and sister Lucy (Susannah Doyle)

Rachel does not get on with her parents. She's had no contact with her father for years; she's never forgiven him for beating up her mother, and she's never forgiven her mother for staying with him. So when they turn up at the wedding, keen to be part of the family, Rachel finds it hard to welcome them. She refuses to let her father give her away, and generally makes it clear that they're not welcome. Pete's speech lets a few cats out of the bag – Rachel's parents did not know, for instance, that their daughter was married. And that's not all, says Rachel. He was black, I had an abortion, and by the way my sister is a lesbian and moved to Australia to get away from you.

Rachel's anger towards her parents never really goes away. When she's reunited with her sister Lucy in Australia, she can't understand why Lucy's trying to build bridges with her father, whom Rachel has dismissed as a worthless bigot. But Lucy's a realist; she wants to maintain a relationship with her parents, and if that means swallowing her pride, she's willing to do it. Rachel could learn a lot from her.

Rod (Gary Sweet)
Jo's father seems like a villain: a rich Sydney businessman who suspects that Pete is nothing but a gold digger. He'd much prefer Jo to marry her old sweetheart Shawn, who's helping him out in the building trade, and he tries every trick in the book to buy Pete off. But eventually he realises that Pete's a good bloke, and he gives the couple his blessing – and a rather nice penthouse as their antipodean holiday home. So he can't be all bad.

Rachel's Other Men

Kris (Lennie James)

The first we hear of Kris Bumstead is when Adam finds his name on an old marriage certificate in one of Rachel's boxes of junk. He assumes, at first, that it's a fake – but Kris is anything but a fake, and much to his surprise Adam discovers that he's just moved in with Mrs Rachel Bumstead. It soon becomes clear that there's unfinished business between Rachel and her first love, whom she met and married at college, only to be deserted within a few days when he ran off with her best friend. She's moved on, she's forgotten about it – or so she says. But when she calls Kris up to Manchester to discuss a divorce, she starts to fall in love with him all over again. They have a shared past, and the attraction is still strong – not least

because Kris is obviously keen to make up for his mistakes. He says he still loves Rachel, and when they go back to the house a drunk Rachel is sick all over his shirt. After this inauspicious beginning, they have sex – without taking any precautions ('Well, I locked the front door,' Rachel tells a horrified Karen). Soon Kris is a permanent fixture at Adam and Rachel's flat, much to Adam's disgust. He's a good cook, a great musician – and he's even good at Twister. Finally both Adam and Rachel pay him off as a way of getting rid of him, and Kris returns to London £1000 better off. But he's left something behind; Rachel's pregnant.

'If I could know exactly what I'd say to you tonight. If I could I wouldn't let you walk away'

Kris writes a song for Rachel

Simon (Stephen Mapes)

Rachel isn't one to let the grass grow under her feet. At the beginning of the pilot she's involved with Simon, an ambitious young professional with a black belt in karate. But Simon puts his job before his relationship, and over a romantic meal in a restaurant he tells Rachel that he's been offered a job in Hong Kong... or, in fact, has already accepted a job in Hong Kong. It's a lot of money, but Rachel's not sure if she's ready to make the move. That's not a problem, says Simon; he'll go on his own. Rachel dumps a bowl of profiteroles over his head in reply. But that's not the end of Simon: the Hong Kong job doesn't work out, and no sooner is he back in Manchester than he's calling on Rachel. His timing is perfect: she's just had a row with Adam, and she jumps straight back into bed with Simon. This leads to the big showdown at the end of the pilot, when Rachel has to choose between her karate-chopping former boyfriend, and her new love who's standing stark naked in the street with a rose stuck up his bum. Tough call...

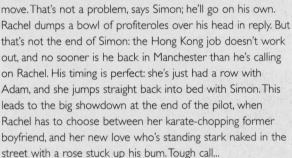

Malcolm Chacksfield
(John Graham Davies)

After her dalliance with young Danny, Rachel switches her attention to Malcolm Chacksfield – Adam's former English teacher, an attractive man in his 40s whom she meets at Adam's school reunion. But what looked like a good catch at the party seems less appealing when he turns up for a date in a bar – dressed like a teacher. Rachel, unable to face him with the fact that she doesn't fancy him, turns on her heels and runs.

Danny (Hugh Dancy)

No sooner does Rachel step back into the office in the second series, than her male co-workers are lining up to take her out. Danny's the front runner: he's younger than Rachel, likes the right movies and has amazing sexual stamina. What starts off as a laddish bet with his colleagues turns out to be a serious involvement for Danny. He even braves meeting Karen and David at breakfast. But, just as Rachel is beginning to think that the age difference is too great, Danny dumps her. It's her friends, he says. He can't stand them.

Nick (Stephen Moyer)

When David's charming and mysterious younger brother Nick turns up unexpectedly at the Marsdens' when Karen and David are out, he starts flirting with their attractive lodger immediately, and Rachel's rather taken with him. But Nick isn't quite as charming as he seems. He's come to Manchester to cadge money off David to pay back a debt. Rachel is blind to Nick's faults, and starts dating him; they have their first kiss under a lamp post liberally strewn with dog turds. Before he leaves, he tells Rachel that he would like to go out with her. This forces Rachel realise that there's really only one man for her, and it ain't Nick.

Jo's Other Men

Suggs (Paterson Joseph)
How can Pete ever hope to date a fitness professional, when he himself is a professional slob? He has a good try, and goes to Jo's aerobics classes, but soon finds himself upstaged by his colleague, Suggs, who pounces on Jo and starts dating her immediately. At first it seems like Suggs is the man for Jo, but after a while the relationship cools, and Jo realises that she's got a great deal more in common with Pete. Suggs may be fit, but Pete wins on personality.

Shawn (Sandy Winton)
He's the reason Jo left Australia in the first place: Shawn and she were engaged, but he would never name a date. In the end, Jo questioned his commitment, and fled to England to escape her disappointment. But Shawn, it seems, has waited for her, and when Jo returns to Sydney with her new fiancé in tow he's determined to get her back. Rod, Jo's father, is on Shawn's side – but Jo stands firm. Pete's the man she wants – for now. Perhaps Shawn will still be waiting when Jo returns to Sydney at the end of the show...

'Not marrying you was the biggest mistake of my life. But I'm ready to put it right. I love you Jo. Marry me.' Shawn tries to win Jo back

Series 5

?? Feb - ?? Mar 2003 6 4 episodes

Pete's back from Australia with Jo as his **wife**, both eager to start a new life in Manchester. But things just don't go their way. At first they have to put up with Pete's mother and her strange **insomniac** ways. And no sooner is she packed off to a suitable residential home (with a big stash to keep her happy) than Pete starts to **suspect** that Jo only married him in order to get a British visa. Nothing Jo can say will stop Pete suspecting the worst, and in the end it drives a wedge between them. Jo goes to a conference in Birmingham, and, after a **drunken party**, sleeps with her colleague, Lee.

After their disastrous Australian trip, David and Karen are living apart. She's not seeing Mark any more, but they've decided to get a **divorce**. And then, to David's astonishment, he finds himself entering into a relationship with his divorce **lawyer**, Robyn - while Karen bumps into Mark again and realises that the old attraction is still as strong as ever. But Mark's not cut out to be a **father**, and the relationship ends. For David, however, Robyn seems to offer a **better future**.

The series starts well for Adam and Rachel and baby Matthew. After a few teething troubles, they're looking forward to living together as a **family** - and they've even managed to buy their own house. But then **disaster strikes**. Rachel is killed in a road accident, leaving Adam - and the rest of the cast - utterly desolate.

There's one little **silver lining** to this cloud. Jenny comes home for the funeral, and gets back together with Pete. So at least someone's happy...

Series 5

Episode 1

Pete and Jo are back... and so is Pete's mother... the Marsden divorce is getting nasty... Ramona's got a new man... and Adam is finding it hard to love baby Matthew.

Pete and Jo are back from Australia, and the whole gang has turned out to greet them. This proves to be something of a surprise for David, who's also arriving at Manchester airport after a business trip to Frankfurt, and can't believe that he's getting such a warm welcome. But he soon learns his mistake; Karen's not there for him, she's there for Pete and Jo. The Marsden marriage is still on the rocks, although Karen's decided, after all, not to stay with Mark. David's living in a rented flat, seeing his children once a week... It's a situation that needs to be resolved, one way or another.

Pete and Jo are overjoyed to be back home, and can't wait to tear back to the flat and start having as much sex as possible. But the honeymoon is short-lived, and reality kicks in soon enough in the shape of Audrey, Pete's mum, who's been evicted from her sheltered accommodation for being too noisy, and comes back to live with her son and new daughter-in-law. It's an awkward situation; Audrey and Jo haven't met, and there's instant rivalry over who comes first in Pete's priorities. Soon enough, Pete and Jo are being woken at 3am by Audrey's nocturnal hoovering. Her arthritis keeps her awake, she says, and hoovering helps her to relax. It's not helping Pete and Jo get used to living together as man and wife.

Rachel and Adam are getting

An unwelcome guest for Pete and Jo.

used to family life. Baby Matthew is now three months old, and Rachel is showing all the signs of turning into an obsessive mother. She doesn't like the idea of Matthew sleeping in his own room, she frets whenever anyone else (including Adam) touches the baby, and she's starting to become agoraphobic, never wanting to leave the house, even to go out for a romantic dinner. And forget about sex: every time Adam goes anywhere near Rachel, she's panicking about Matthew. Before long Adam's banished to the nursery, sleepless with frustration and jealousy. It seems that the baby is coming between Adam and Rachel - and Adam's finding it hard to love his son in the way he wants to.

Karen runs into Mark in a bookshop; she's not seen him for three months, since she walked away from him in Australia, and she's not sure that she ought to see him at all; she's got other things to worry about, like the divorce, which she and David are trying to keep as amicable as possible. But the moment they meet, it's clear that the attraction is as strong as ever, and soon they're meeting up for clandestine coffees. Mark advises Karen to get her own lawyer to handle the divorce; if she accepts David's offer of their usual solicitor, she won't stand a chance. And so Marsden vs Marsden takes a turn for the worst.

David, meanwhile, has sacrificed his usual lawyer to Karen, and instead engages the services of Robyn Duff - who, to his surprise, turns out to be not a man but a woman, and a very attractive one at that. She can't understand why David's being so nice to his wife: after all, he might just as well cite her adultery as grounds for divorce as she's citing his. And then there's the question of custody: does he really want his children to go to a women who has a history of alcoholism? Suddenly the amicable divorce is turning very ugly indeed.

The only ray of sunshine is a budding romance between Ramona

A new woman for David.

'I know David's free to see other people. But his divorce lawyer?'

Karen's not impressed

and Lee, a swimming instructor she's met at the posh health club where she takes Josh and the twins. Lee's an accomplished flirt - it goes with the job - but Ramona's determined to get her hands on him. First of all she needs health club membership, which she manages to wangle out of David in return for information about Karen and Mark.

Pete and Jo are finding married life hard going. Audrey is keeping them awake every night, until Jo finds the perfect solution to all their problems. Marijuana is supposed to provide effective relief from arthritis; all they need to do is get their hands on some. Adam knows the right connections, and sends them off to a minicab firm somewhere on the outskirts of town, where a friendly old dealer called Grandad sells Audrey a bag of grass at special pensioners' rates. Pete walks in on Jo and Audrey sitting in the living room smoking dope - and he's even more shocked when his mother passes him the joint.

Rachel and Adam's marriage is going from bad to worse. Things are so miserable at home that Adam's taking to nipping into pubs and chatting up

Can Ramona tame Lee?

Mini-Matt takes over, much to
Adam's chagrin.

women in the park. "It's like Rachel died giving birth and this stranger took her place," he tells Pete. He's even started having conversations with the baby, a malignant miniature adult he calls "Mini-Matt", who's deliberately coming between him and his wife. It all becomes too much for Adam at the naming ceremony when, after hearing some touching words from Pete - the very words that Adam read out at Adam Junior's christening in series one, written by Pete's dad - he admits to everyone that he doesn't love his son, that fatherhood doesn't feel good. He storms out and Rachel follows him, to admit that the reason she's so paranoid is because she once dropped him on the floor and is now consumed by guilt. They realise that the baby doesn't need to be wrapped in cotton wool - and, later that night, they resume sexual relations.

Pete and Jo are finally on their own; a mellow Audrey has moved into some new sheltered accommodation, where she's made a lot of new friends - who come round to her room every night for a relaxing smoke.

Episode 2

Lee and Ramona are on a roll...Pete and Jo are heading for trouble... Rachel's back at work and Adam's going to singing groups with Matthew... David and Robyn grow closer.

Ramona's romance with Lee from the health club is progressing slowly but surely. They've been out for a drink together, and he's wooing her with gifts of sexy underwear, but Ramona wants to keep him hanging a little bit longer; she doesn't want to be just another notch on his bedpost. Lee's got a reputation for sleeping with all the women he meets at the gym, and Ramona wants more than a one-night stand.

There's trouble afoot for Jo and Pete: the immigration authorities are suspicious of their marriage, and want them to come in to the office to prove that it wasn't just done to secure a visa. But how can they prove that it's a real marriage? None of the household bills have Jo's name on, and Pete's somehow managed to tape football over his only copy of the wedding video. Their first interrogation by the immigration officials goes well enough - but a seed of doubt has been sown in Pete's mind. Did Jo really marry him for love? Or was there an ulterior motive?

All change for Adam and Rachel: he's been made redundant, and she fancies going back to work. So suddenly Adam finds himself in the role of the househusband and full-time father,

Ramona can't resist Lee's charms. And neither, it seems, can anyone else.

a job that he finds it hard to adjust to. Rachel is shocked at how easily she slips back into work - and doesn't think about Matthew for hours at a time. Before long she has an overnight trip to Milan to plan - and that means leaving Adam holding the baby. He soon realises that parenthood carries some serious responsibilities: not least taking Matthew to well-intentioned but absolutely hideous singing groups with other parents who have children called Tallulah.

Karen and David's divorce proceedings are getting more and more acrimonious. Robyn advises him to sue for guardianship of the children, and to do everything in his power to keep his money under control; in many divorces, she tells him, husbands lose the children and end up paying over £100,000 a year to the ex-wife. David goes along with it, and sends a valuer round to the marital home. This just winds Karen up even more, so she ups the ante by increasing the amount of her maintenance evaluation. Things are getting out of control - not least because both Karen and David are starting new relationships and feeling bitter about the marriage. Increasingly, the children are being used as pawns - and Josh in particular is starting to suffer.

David's professional relationship with Robyn suddenly spills over into personal territory when, after a night in a bar, they end up staying the night together at her place. David feels guilty and unhappy, but when he realises that he's a free man and that Robyn really likes him, he's happy to continue. Meanwhile Karen is playing it cool with Mark; she still loves him, but she is wary

about letting him stay the night until he's accepted his responsibilities towards her children. But Mark's adamant: he wants Karen, not her children.

Ramona finally relents and lets Lee stay the night; it's just what he's been waiting for, and for a while it seems as if they're made for each other. But Lee's got a roving eye, and Ramona's made it quite clear that she won't stand for any kind of infidelity.

Pete's getting more and more worried about Jo's motives for marrying him.

'Good-looking birds trade up, not down. Unelss he's bloody rich.'

Pete confronts Jo

A chance remark that she'd once asked Lee to marry her - in jest - sends Pete scurrying off to read Jo's private emails. And he gets what he deserves: confirmation (or so it seems) that Jo was looking for a man to save her from deportation when Pete just happened to come along. She didn't really fancy him, it seems - she was just looking for a husband. Pete, always quick to believe the worst, jumps to conclusions, and their marriage is headed towards the rocks.

Rachel returns from her overnight trip to Milan to find Adam bored and frustrated with parenthood. He's even gone so far as getting interviewed for a new job - and, despite the fact that he had a baby with a dirty nappy on his knee at the time, he gets the position.

Karen and David's divorce reaches the crunch point. David's furious because he found Mark looking after the children, with Josh in tears - and he immediately assumes that Mark has somehow hurt him. Suddenly there's talk of restraining orders as the lawyers whip their clients into a frenzy. Karen confronts Mark over his

Marsden vs Marsden takes a turn for the worse.

treatment of Josh, and gives him an ultimatum: love me, love my kids. Mark can't accept it, and they part for ever.

At a legal conference the next day, Karen and David realise that all the bitterness in their divorce is the result of communicating through lawyers. Neither really wants to hurt the other, and they decide, to their lawyers' horror, to return to their original plan of an amicable split. David, chastened by the experience, ends his relationship with Robyn - for now, at least.

Pete's convinced that Jo only married him for a visa, and confronts her with his "proof". And despite all her assurances to the contrary, he walks out on their marriage. There's a partial reconciliation at the end of the episode, but it's clear that any trust that existed between Pete and Jo has been fatally undermined.

Episode 3 (written by Mike Bullen and Matt Greenhalgh)

Rachel and Adam are buying a house... So's David... Jo makes a big mistake... Adam has an unwelcome visitor... David wants Karen back... tragedy strikes!

Life couldn't get much better for Adam and Rachel.

Rachel and Adam are both working now, and Matthew's spending the day with a child minder. At last they seem to be getting parenthood into perspective, and life is settling down into a pleasant pattern. Until, that is, Rachel discovers that the house they live in, that they've been renting since they first got together, is on the market. A little investigation reveals that the previous owner has died of a heart attack, leaving behind him a trail of bad debts, and the house is to be auctioned to pay off his creditors. Rachel wants to carry on living there - but in the years since they moved in, property prices in Didsbury have gone through the roof, and even with two of them working they can't afford to live in their own home. And so they start, reluctantly, house-hunting.

Things aren't going so well for Pete and Jo; they're sleeping in separate beds, their marriage seemingly in tatters. She's got her visa problems sorted, but what's the point of staying if she's not talking to her own husband? When one of her colleagues suggests that she comes to a sales conference in Birmingham, Jo jumps at the idea; anything would be welcome to get away from the tension at home. But before she goes, she makes one final effort to patch things up with Pete by buying him a Chinese takeaway - and, coincidentally, he's had the same idea, and has cooked her a spaghetti bolognaise. That's all it takes to get them back on track.

'You honestly think a cheap bunch of flowers is going to make the little lady happy?'

Robyn loses patience with David

David is trying hard to avoid Robyn, although she's still handling his divorce. He feels guilty for allowing his personal feelings for Robyn to embitter divorce proceedings with Karen, and so every time she calls he pretends to be in a meeting. Finally she confronts him in his office and gives him his marching orders; David doesn't like being put on the spot, and reacts badly. So that would appear to be that.

Rachel and Adam have an unexpected visitor: Bill, Adam's father, who would like to get to know his grandson. Adam's furious: he's never forgiven Bill for walking out on him and his mother when he was just a kid - and he's cross with Rachel, too, for letting Bill know that he was a grandfather. Bill tries to explain, but Adam throws him out - and Bill's left with nowhere to stay in Manchester. Karen comes to the rescue, and puts him up in her house for a few days, hoping that she can bring father and son back together. And there's another reason for her charity: she finds Bill rather attractive...

Rachel gets drawn in as the go-between, and agrees to meet Bill for a drink. He persuades her to let him have one final attempt at speaking to Adam, and so she takes him home. Adam reacts with his usual rage, until Bill finally manages to tell him his side of the story: he had to leave home because Adam's mother found out that he was having an affair - with a man. She prevented him from having any future contact with his son, and Bill has regretted it ever since. Adam's pig-headed at first, but relents and goes for a drink with his father - and, thanks to the miracle of beer, they manage a spot of father-son bonding.

Tragedies

☆ Rachel's fatal car crash was filmed in Moston, just outside Manchester. It was a big production number, involving a stunt truck driver and two stunt car drivers. Rachel's car was completely written off – and a dummy played the part of Rachel!

☆ The paramedics who attended the scene were the real thing.

David realises that he's made a big mistake with Karen, and tries to win her back with flowers and chocolate. It doesn't work, or so it seems: even his calls and emails go unanswered. Finally Robyn turns up in David's office and slaps a non-molestation order on his desk - which, on closer inspection, turns out to be an invitation to dinner. They quickly resume sexual relations, and seem to be growing very close. Robyn, naturally, thinks it's time she met David's friends.

Jo has gone to Birmingham to enjoy herself at the conference. She's in ebullient spirits: her marriage is sorted, her visa is sorted, now at last she can have some fun. This entails drinking huge quantities of tequila and ending up in bed with Lee - who, let us not forget, is now officially going out with Ramona. She's so consumed with guilt when she returns to Manchester that she confesses all to Karen - never a good move. Lee responds quite differently. Convinced that he can have his cake and eat it too, he asks Ramona to move in with him. Is it true love? Or does he just like having his laundry done?

Adam and Rachel have found a house: not much of a house, but it's all they can afford, and Adam tries to persuade Rachel that it will be fine with a lick of paint. But Bill realises that Rachel really hates it, and offers to lend Adam the money to buy the house they're currently living in. Adam leaps into action: the auction is today, and there's no time to lose. He races round to the sales rooms, and finds that he's bidding against David. When David realises that his plan to turn a quick profit has been rumbled, he pulls out of the bidding and allows Adam to win the day.

Rachel didn't stand a chance against the huge lorry.

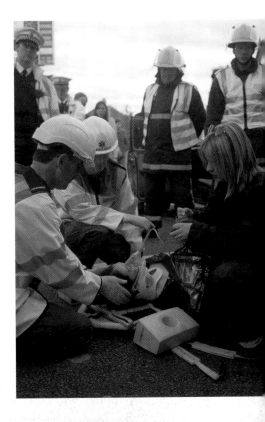

The house seems to be in the bag - but first Adam needs a deposit. He calls Rachel and tells her to get round there quick. But the traffic's bad, and she's late. No matter: David's stumped up the money as a peace offering.

Rachel's cursing at the traffic when Adam calls her to tell her that the house is hers. She's overjoyed, puts the phone down - and doesn't see the truck speeding towards her car.

As the emergency services cut Rachel from the wreckage, a policeman answers her phone. It's Karen calling to congratulate her...

The news spreads fast, and the gang gather at the hospital where Rachel has been taken with massive head injuries. Adam watches as she dies.

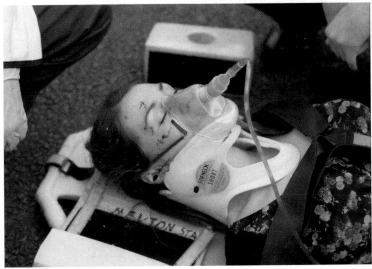

Episode 4

Jenny's back... Adam thinks he's coping... but his friends know better... Karen is falling to pieces... and David is there to hold her hand... Pete and Jo are finished... Ramona and Lee are finished... Pete and Jenny decide to try again.

Adam's preparing for Rachel's funeral - but, to him, she doesn't really seem to be dead. Everywhere he goes, everything he does, he hears her voice and sees her face. She's still with him and not letting go until he's ready to make it on his own.

The loss of Rachel leaves everybody devastated.

'Bogie and Bergmann will always have Paris. Raich and I will always have Port Meirion.'

Adam scatters Rachel's ashes

Jenny arrives for the funeral in a limo, heavily pregnant. Everyone asks her about the father, but she's evasive; all they know is that if she can afford to ride around in limos, she must be doing pretty well. At the funeral, all Rachel's friends speak of their love for her. Adam plays 'I've Got You Under My Skin' - the song with which he originally wooed Rachel all those years ago with a rose stuck up his bum.

Jenny's got nowhere to stay in Manchester, and so Jo, in a drunken moment, tells her that she can come and stay with her and Pete. Adam, meanwhile, still has his father Bill staying with him, and Karen's got Ramona back; she's not happy with the way that Lee is flirting with all the female clients, and has decided that he's not worthy of her.

Adam's determined to get over his loss, and goes back to work way too soon, telling everyone that he's fine. He thinks he can start getting on with his life, and tries to return to his old bachelor ways, chatting up women and drinking with the lads. But it's a false dawn, and the strain is beginning to show. Adam's boss sends him home indefinitely before he cracks up completely.

Karen's finding it hard to cope with her friend's death; a piece of her youth has died with Rachel, and it just brings home to her what a mess she's made of her life. She breaks down in tears in the supermarket, and goes home with a bottle of red wine. But instead of drinking it, she phones David, who drops everything and rushes round to comfort Karen. Their marriage may be over, but David and Karen are still very close - and, fortunately for David, Robyn understands where his priorities lie.

Pete's finding it strange having his

Karen wouldn't have made it through the funeral without David.

two wives under one roof. Jo's trying to be reasonable, but it's clear to her that Pete and Jenny have a shared history that she can never compete with. As Pete and Jenny draw closer in the aftermath of Rachel's death, Jo feels herself squeezed out. And the guilt of her one-night stand with Lee is beginning to eat away at her.

Lee knows no such remorse. His solution to Ramona's departure is simple: he asks her to marry him. No more flirting, he promises: in the future, she's the only woman for him. Ramona is delighted; this must mean that Lee is serious about her. But Karen's not so easily fooled; she sees Lee hanging around Jo, and realises that there's more to this than just a professional friendship. Should she warn Ramona?

Adam's friends are worried about him, and one by one they turn up at the house to check up on him. Adam's response is to hide away upstairs with the baby, talking to Rachel, until he loses patience and throws everyone out. He doesn't need them to tell him how to grieve, he says; he's doing fine on his own. But he's not, and a breakdown is on the way. When he sees Matthew crawling for the first time, he realises that this is something Rachel will never witness, and that Matthew will never know his mother. For the first time, he cries. He calls up Karen and she rushes round to comfort him.

Jenny realises that she's coming between Pete and Jo, and so she moves in with Adam; she's always been his comfort in times of trouble, and now they both need each other. She's alone too: the father of her child was her boss in New York, and as soon as he discovered she was pregnant he wanted nothing more to do with her. So she's come back to Manchester without a job, without a home and without a boyfriend. Adam's solution is impulsive: she can move in with him. Just as friends, of course, but they could see how it goes...

Karen accidentally tells Ramona about her suspicions regarding Lee - and so Ramona storms off with murderous intention. She confronts Jo and gives her an enormous black eye - and that's the end of that. It's also the end of Jo's marriage; Pete realises that his suspicions weren't unfounded, and he can never trust his wife again.

While Ramona stays home to nurse the children and a broken heart, the rest

> ### Star Turn
>
> ⑥ Due to Fay Ripley's pregnancy, episode four was filmed before episode three.
>
> ⑥ At the end of the Port Meirion sequence, James Nesbitt had to fly to New York for the premiere of his new film, *Bloody Sunday*. A helicopter picked him up from a field adjacent to the location, then swooped down to the cast and crew who were still filming by the sea. James gave a regal wave, and he was off to the airport.

of the gang heads off to Port Meirion to scatter Rachel's ashes. It was here that Matthew was conceived, and it was a place that Rachel loved. It's a time for some home truths. Jo tells Adam that she's destroyed her own marriage by sleeping with Lee. Pete tells Jenny that his marriage is over; she tells him that Adam's asked her to move in with him. Pete confronts Adam: just when he and Jenny have a chance to become a family again, Adam's just waiting to steal Jenny away. David and Karen, meanwhile, seem to be becoming closer again.

Early the next morning, the friends gather to scatter Rachel's ashes - or what's left of them. After Pete's dropped the casket in the pub, and Matthew's tipped them over in the living room, and Adam's lost half of them in the back of the car, there's only a tiny trickle of dust to throw to the winds.

Pete and Jo return to Manchester where he tells her he wants a divorce. She decides to return to Australia; there's nothing left for her in England, and she would rather walk away from her mistakes. So Jo moves out - and Jenny moves back in, with Adam Junior. The Giffords are a family again.

David has to choose between Karen and Robyn, between a past that he knows all too well and an uncertain future. It's a hard call: but he chooses Robyn. Karen is left alone with Ramona to look after the children.

And for Adam? He can't stay in the home that was once his and Rachel's. And so he leaves Manchester for good, with his father.

SC 13

INT. CREMATORIUM. DAY. 1 (MON) 1105

ADAM, JO, PETE, KAREN, DAVID, JENNY, MARY BRADLEY, BRIAN
BRADLEY, BABY MATTHEW, ADAM'S DAD (BILL), OFFICIAL

RACHEL'S COFFIN IS CENTRE STAGE ON A RAISED DAIS. THE
ASSEMBLED GUESTS SIT ON BENCHES, FACING THE COFFIN. IN THE
FRONT ROW SIT (IN ORDER FROM THE AISLE): JO, PETE, ADAM
(HOLDING MATTHEW), JENNY, DAVID AND KAREN. BEHIND ADAM
SITS HIS FATHER. KAREN IS CRYING HEAVILY, COMFORTED BY
DAVID. JENNY AND JO ARE WIPING THEIR EYES. JENNY AND PETE
SUPPORT ADAM, BUT FOR THE MOMENT HE'S HOLDING IT TOGETHER;
HE'S CLOSED DOWN HIS EMOTIONS. BESIDE THE COFFIN IS A
PODIUM, AT WHICH STANDS THE OFFICIAL WHO'S CONDUCTING THE
SECULAR FUNERAL SERVICE. HE SPEAKS INTO A MICROPHONE.

OFFICIAL

Some of Rachel's friends and family will now say a few
words about her. First, her closest friend, Karen Marsden.

THE OFFICIAL STEPS BACK. KAREN RISES FROM HER SEAT AND
WALKS SLOWLY TO THE PODIUM. SHE'S BARELY HOLDING IT
TOGETHER AND IT'S A MOMENT OR TWO BEFORE SHE CAN TRUST
HERSELF TO SPEAK WITHOUT BREAKING DOWN.

KAREN

Rachel and I grew up together. Not that we knew each
other as kids. But when we met we seemed so much
younger...

KAREN CAN BARELY CONTINUE, BUT FINALLY MANAGES.

KAREN (cont'd)

We'd go out together after work, on the trawl we called
it...

KAREN BREAKS DOWN IN TEARS. HER FRIENDS CAST NERVOUS
GLANCES TO EACH OTHER. DAVID CAN'T STAND TO SEE HER
SUFFERING, SO LEAPS TO HER SIDE AND HOLDS HER, ENCOURAGING
HER TO TRY AGAIN. HE WHISPERS TO HER.

DAVID

Go on.

BUT KAREN CAN'T DO IT. SHE SHAKES HER HEAD AND CRIES INTO
DAVID'S SHOULDER. HE HOLDS HER AGAINST HIM, THEN SPEAKS
INTO THE MICROPHONE.

DAVID (cont'd)

Rachel was a beautiful person. Looks, personality. And what was best about her:... she didn't know it. She was told often enough - by Adam, her friends - but she wouldn't have it.

BESIDE DAVID, KAREN NODS - THAT'S THE RACHEL SHE REMEMBERS.

DAVID SMILES, WARMED BY THE MEMORY OF RACHEL.

DAVID (cont'd)

That makes her sound perfect. She wasn't of course. But you forgave her any shortcomings because they were so outweighed.

DISSOLVE TO SC 14 INT CREMATORIUM:

INT. CREMATORIUM. DAY. 1 (MON) 1115

ADAM, JO, PETE, KAREN, DAVID, JENNY, MARY BRADLEY, BRIAN BRADLEY, BABY MATTHEW, BILL, OFFICIAL

DAVID AND KAREN'S PLACE AT THE PODIUM HAS BEEN TAKEN BY PETE. DAVID IS BACK IN HIS SEAT, COMFORTING KAREN.

PETE

She owed me a tenner.

THERE'S A SLIGHT MOMENT OF DOUBT AT THIS REMARK THEN ADAM LAUGHS OUT LOUD IN THE FRONT ROW. PETE SMILES. A BEAT.

PETE (cont'd)

If not for Rachel, I'd've missed the birth of my son. I was on a golf course,

(nods in direction of David)

with David, when suddenly we see this Mini tearing up the fairway. Literally! Rachel to the rescue. The members weren't happy, but I was delighted; well, I was losing. Anyway, we made it in time.

(to coffin)

Thanks, Raich.

CUT TO SC 15 INT CREMATORIUM:

INT. CREMATORIUM. DAY. 1 (MON) 1117

ADAM, JO, PETE, KAREN, DAVID, JENNY, MARY BRADLEY, BRIAN BRADLEY, BABY MATTHEW, BILL, OFFICIAL

PETE SWAPS PLACES AT THE PODIUM WITH JENNY.

JENNY

I've been away the past year. New York. You get homesick. Friends say they'll write but, well, we're all busy, aren't we? Rachel wrote. Emails. Two, three times a week. About Matthew. Adam. She loved you guys.

ADAM, HOLDING MATT, SMILES HIS APPRECIATION AT JENNY.

JENNY (cont'd)

She loved life. I'd come home some days, feeling a bit down. I'd log on and there she'd be, jabbering away... She always cheered me up.

DISSOLVE TO SC 16 INT CREMATORIUM:

INT. CREMATORIUM. DAY. 1 (MON) 1120

ADAM, JO, PETE, KAREN, DAVID, JENNY, MARY BRADLEY, BRIAN BRADLEY, BABY MATTHEW, BILL, OFFICIAL, RACHEL

ADAM STEPS UP TO THE PODIUM. JENNY IS NOW HOLDING MATTHEW. ADAM TAKES A LONG MOMENT TO COMPOSE HIMSELF.

ADAM

It's a pity the one person who'd enjoy this the most can't be here.

(beat)

Except, of course, she is...

ADAM LOOKS AT THE COFFIN. RACHEL IS STANDING BESIDE IT. ADAM SMILES.

ADAM (cont'd)

I can see her now. I'm sure you can too. If you can't, just take a look at our son. Matthew's smile, the sparkle in his eyes, the look of grim determination you sometimes see on his face - they all come from Rachel... We thought we couldn't have children. Matthew was our gift. Her gift to me. I'm sorry he'll never have the chance to know his Mum. And his Dad's best friend.

(smiles at Rachel)

I will miss you, girl.

RACHEL NODS: SHE KNOWS THAT. IN THE FRONT ROW, EVERYONE LOOKS A BIT GUTTED. PETE WIPES AWAY A SILENT TEAR.